SET for Success

Self-Evolutionary Templates for Success

by

David A. Jacobi

Personal Edition

Published by David A. Jacobi, Inc.

267 Carlton Ave., Piscataway, NJ 08854-3056

(732) 968-1473

book@setforsuccess.com

www.setforsuccess.com

Tracy and Gerald
unable to come but I hope
you guys celebrate for the
rest of your lives
David Jacobi

ISBN: 0-9667377-0-9

Library of Congress Catalog Number 98-96629

"SET for Success" is a trademark of David A. Jacobi

Edited by Tom Costello
Word Association Publishers
and
Sandy Carpenter
Live Oak Productions

Cover Designed by Sandy Carpenter
Live Oak Productions

This publication includes image #054077 from CorelDraw
which is protected by the copyright laws of the USA, Canada,
and elsewhere. Used under license.

Published November 1998

Printed in the United States of America

The Self-Evolutionist

Fire was instilled in the human breast

by the maker of the universe.

It was created by nature alone

until we learned to strike a stone.

Soon we evolved and were surely blessed

learned how thoughts could be caressed.

Projected images in the time to come

linguistic thinking replaced being dumb.

By image and word our thoughts described

needed resources came in with the tide.

Now we are able to strike fire in our souls

to guide us forward toward our goals.

The fire of passion to perform our best

the fire to live, as Self-Evolutionists.

David A. Jacobi   1998

Dedication

For those who feel that the universe has given them the right to be the best that they can be; for those who are determined to be, the best that they can be; for those who have dedicated themselves to life, or God, or a mission; who want to become self evolutionist; this book is dedicated to you.

For those who are returning to humanity after a period of disillusionment; who desire to live where people are not shunned because they seem to be different, who are too honest and not political enough to fit in, who trust in their beliefs and values even when different from the self-appointed gods of decorum and power; this book is especially dedicated to you.

For those who are not sure but would like to believe that the universe has given them the right to be the best that they can be; for those who are dubious but suspect they would like to dedicate themselves to life, or God, or a mission; who may want to become self evolutionist; this book is especially dedicated to you.

Contents

The Self-Evolutionist   iii

Dedication   iv

We Are   1

Look Forward   11

What is Your Reality? 11
My Responsibility 13
Your Responsibility 13
Success or Failure 14
Self Image 14
Self Help Books 15
This Book 17
Beliefs, Decisions, and Strategies 17
Self-Evolutionary Templates 18
The Self-Evolutionary Process 18
A Generic Process 18
Thoughts About Change 19
How to Use This Book 19
Thoughts are Valuable 20
Look to the Future 20
Endnotes 20

Part One   21

Preview of the Process   23

The Self-Evolutionary Process 23

Look Backward   25

Look to the Past 25
The Universe 26
The Big Bang 26
The Solar System 27
The Earth 27
Humankind 27
    Bipedalism 28
    Homo Erectus. 30
    Temporal-Sequential Activities 31

Modern Humans 32
The Process Defined 36
Endnotes 36

Look Inward   37

What is Consciousness? 37
Conscious Awareness/Unconscious Awareness. . . . 38
Learning and Thinking 38
The Awareness Point of View 42
What Awareness Brings 44
Power of the Unconscious 44
The Process Further Defined 45
Endnotes 46

Mental Tools   47

Monitoring Thoughts 48
Multiple Thoughts 48
One Thing at a Time. 49
Some Definitions 49
Ideas in Space. 51
Creating Subjective Experience 51
Dividing Time and Space. 52
Subjective Experience 53
Sensory Modalities. 53
Your Favorite Sensory System. 57
Get in Touch. 58
Sensory Sequencing 58
Enhancing Subjective Experience 59
Sensory Adjustments 59
Enhance Your Feelings. 60
Generate Strong Images 62
Generate Good Internal Dialogue. 62
Associate Subjective Experience 64
Simple Associations. 65
Spatial Associations 66
Project Subjective Experience 67
Time 67
Establishing Your Time Concept 69
View Time and Envision Time. 69
Draw Your Time Concept 69
Project into the Future 70
Assumptions 70
The Process Further Defined 72

Endnotes 73

Part Two 75

Overview 77

What is Success? 78
The Self-Evolutionary Components 80
The Self-Evolutionary Process 83
    Design a Template 84
    Implement the Template. 84
    As a System 85
The Process Further Defined 86

Design Your Self-Evolutionary Template 87

What is Reality? 87
Entertain Ideas 88
Qualify an Idea 90
    A Good Goal. 90
    In a Secure Manner. 91
    Original Intentions/Derived Gains 92
    Of Your Own Volition 93
    Sensory Based 94
    Using Positive Language 94
Believe 97
    What are Beliefs? 98
    Use a Reference Belief. 99
Decide 103
    Decision Analysis. 104
Choose a Strategy 109
Project the Goal 114
    Director's View 114
    Actor's View 115
    Make the Projection 115
    Re-evaluate the Goal 116
Project the Effects 118
Perform Rehearsal 120
Analyze the Results 123
    Repetition Counts. 123
The Rubber Meets the Road 125
Reality Score Card 127
Endnotes 127

Implement Your Self-Evolutionary Template 129

Balance 129
The Implementation Process 131

State of Mind 131
Self-Evolutionary Components 132
Implementing a Template 132
Reality Score Card 133
Epilog 134

Design Sheets   135

Spatial Associations   149

Summary   161
Look Forward 161
Look Backward 161
Look Inward 162
Mental Tools 162
Overview 163
Design Your Self-Evolutionary Template 163
Implement Your Self-Evolutionary Template 163

Appendix   165
Brain Function 165
Lateralization 166
    The Left Hemisphere 166
    The Right Hemisphere 169
Making a Difference 172
How Associations Work 173
Endnotes 174

About the Author   175

Feedback   177

Order Form   179

Index   181

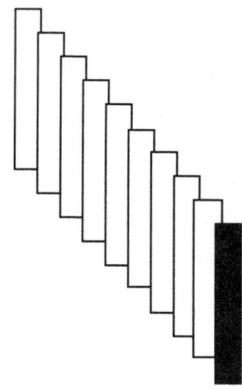

We Are

When I was beginning *SET for Success*, taking some notes, peering into my memories and reflecting on what is essential for success, I intuitively began to think about evolution, where we came from, how we came to be as we are. I reflected on how we take one step after another, speak one word after another, how we use all five senses plus language to survive and prosper. How our ancestors came down out of the rain forest, sailed the oceans, and how we eventually flew to the moon should provide insight for us to use to become more successful.

All species try to spread to all available niches; that's part of evolution. We ended up at the top of the food chain, filling all available niches, and now look toward the planets to extend our range. The success story of the human race provides clues as to how we as individuals can be more successful and is explained later in this book.

The fossilized remains that the Leakeys and other scientist studied, the missing links looked for, and the numerous theories of evolution presented are all intriguing to me. After some time, while in a meditative state searching for language about the "essence of success," a thought came, it titillated, and then thrilled me.

"We are human evolution"

We develop from a single cell that gestates for nine months, taking on the different shapes of our evolution in the process, and are then born a complete human being with the genetic blueprint for success installed. We are the human success story that has taken 5 to 10 million years to tell. The story of mankind is in our muscles, bones, sinew; in every cell of our being in the form of DNA, the intellectual center of all cells. The atoms of our body originally came from the stars but are now arranged according to DNA instructions that make up the "design" of our being.

We are success

The thinking that created the Sumerian culture in the fertile crescent (the Cradle of Civilization) between the Tigris and Euphrates rivers is embedded in our genes. The intelligence that they used to create irrigation systems, the first cereal agriculture (barley and wheat), the earliest writings (Cuneiform), the wheel, a math system based on the numeral 60, and a banking system is part of us. The intelligence that created the Egyptian, Greek, and Roman civilizations is embedded in us right now in the form of DNA. The intelligence that created the Sistine Chapel is in the gene pool that we draw from as we journey through life. So why doesn't success come more easily for us. We have a tremendous amount of programming in our DNA and almost all of it is pointed toward success. Why does achievement often turn into such a struggle.

The fog sets in

At birth we enter a world of conflicting ideas; conflicting agendas. A kind of fog sets in that is sometimes difficult to see and identify; it requires an objective eye to separate it from what is real. It is similar to what many spiritual paths in the Far East refer to as "maya," the illusionary appearance of the world. We are taught that we are a product of both nature and nurture; (our DNA and the environment that we live in). Our environment is this great country with land owned by its citizens, farm to farm, town to town, coast to coast, with millions of people promoting different ideas and agendas. We live in a democracy, the best form of government in the world but we need our own thinking strategies to look after our own interests. We need to adapt to our environment in an intelligent manner so that we do well for ourselves and our families.

Part of the maya is that we have so many people, churches, schools, and other organizations teaching us what "not to do" but we don't have enough teaching us what "to do." You will see how this can be remedied later in this book using the Self-Evolutionary process.

We as a nation have developed robustly, both technically and economically, and in many ways culturally but this is also a harsh environment. The economic pie isn't being divided equally. Corporations have been having record profits but employee wages have not been keeping pace. In many cases wages have been falling behind. Both parents have been working longer and harder for the same or less money, struggling to maintain their standard of living. There isn't enough time to bring up the kids the way that they would like so "too much" is left to the schools who have some fog of their own. And and too many of the kids don't want to learn anyway.

The real problem is that we don't have a challenge

It might be more accurate to say that we, as a nation and as individuals, don't have a challenge that we are willing to accept. There are plenty of challenges. Our K-12 education ranks around twentieth globally and there is no way that we can maintain our standard of living and have a great nation with such mediocrity. We have plenty of challenges with crime, health care, and the general attitude of the American people. Our emigrant forebears had a "fire in their vision" that seems to have dimmed, and for many, gone out. It is up to each of us to move forward, to be more successful, and I will show you how.

Not having a challenge is a problem because the human spirit, the DNA in the heart, brain, and bones is somehow programmed to do best when challenged. It provides the compass for human evolution. Someone wrote a letter to the editorial section of the New York Times in 1995. The letter described an experiment by a group of psychologists. They took some birds to a desert island and provided them with a perfect environment; food, water, foliage; everything was exactly what these particular birds thrived on. The psychologists then scientifically monitored the birds and observed some unusual behavior. Instead of enjoying the island they began to fight and squabble for no obvious reason. There was plenty of food yet they fought over it and pecked holes in each other's eggs.

The study was said to illustrate the fact that living things need challenges to be healthy. Play God for a minute. If you want living things to evolve you could put a genetic mechanism in them so that if they are **not** challenged, if they are **not** striving to get better, they will be dissatisfied and not do well. If they are challenged and meet the challenge, they will flourish. We are genetically programmed for success. We only need to align our thinking with our genetic programming and challenge ourselves instead of poking holes in each other's eggs. I will show you how using a Self-Evolutionary template.

We have always had challenges: we learned to control fire, to cook, to keep warm, and to scare wild animals away. We made weapons to protect us and tools to cut our meat and grind the corn that we grew. We also learned to project our visions into the future well enough to sail the oceans and invent the light bulb, the telescope, and build the pyramids. The challenges continue to come and we can continue to meet them if we choose to. If not immediately, after analysis and renewed effort; within the cybernetic model of using feedback as a control mechanism; but we need the will, we need the determination.

Using this point of view, politicians could challenge their rivals to find better ideas instead of poking holes in their opponents personalties and then the voters could vote for the person with the best ideas. The person willing to accept challenges and move the country ahead might win the election. The country could then continue to evolve instead of declining. We are trying to impeach a president for having an affair and lying about it while health care in this country is a crime. Sure it's important to teach kids to tell the truth but we are teaching them not to lie. There is a difference which I explain later. But first, imagine young children continually being told what "not" to do rather than what "to" do. Give children an afternoon to **not** do things. Imagine how confused they would feel. The brain has difficulty handling negatives yet parents and teachers use them more often than not when trying to discipline. All of the "thou shalt nots" should be turned into instructions for performing positive deeds. Finding fault is necessary, we have to hold people accountable but when that is the whole focus of the country rather than growing educationally, technically, and in wisdom (enriching the human spirit), we are not a great nation.

Television the giant focus

The reticular formation in the brain stem is a valve that let's more or less information in from the five senses. It, along with other brain circuitry adjusts for too much stimulation (when the fire alarm sounds) or too little stimulation (when we meditate) so that we can have some balance in the way we ingest information. This also provides more choice in what we pay attention to. The television commercials come on with an explosion and then the information is blasted at us with the beat of drums and other crashing sounds, all at scientifically determined frequency and rhythm to overwhelm the reticular formation. The commercials are designed to overwhelm our sensibilities and install messages in our brains that we might not want. It's brain washing, pure and simple and the number of them makes me wonder if there will be any television programs in the future or will television be strictly commercials, all played loudly. Are we headed for a world of maya and nothing real.

Television focuses, magnifies, and extends our problems. Focuses on the negative in most cases rather than the positive. As landlords of the air waves we should be able to watch television without getting our brains slammed and our thoughts manipulated. But with all of the information that keeps being generated and disseminated and all of the conflicting agendas vying for our attention and money, who can keep track, and after a while, who cares. If the American people turned off their televisions in protest for a day or two, the television industry would cry for relief; but who is to make the revolution?

The saddest part

The saddest part for me is that some of the worst behavior in our culture is put up on the television screen and therefore emulated. That's how the human mind works, it looks out at the world and models what it sees. That's how we learned to walk and talk as kids and that's where we get much of our direction from as adults. If it weren't true, if it didn't work that way, the advertising industry would collapse and kids might stop killing kids. Thank heaven for the Mark McGwires and Sammy Sosas but they are being overshadowed by murder and mayhem on the television.

A kid who got into a gun fight in California not long ago was hit in the arm with a slug from someone's gun. He couldn't understand why it hurt. (It didn't hurt on tv.) We program our kids to be violent, put them in situations that they don't see any way out of, and then get angry when they oblige us. It isn't fair to the kids, it is counter productive for the nation, and it's an evolutionary blight on the human race. You don't have to be in a gunfight in this nation today to be numbed up and dumbed down until you don't know when it hurts. This unreal world of television that is presented to kids and adults alike is part of the maya that keeps confusing us. We as a nation and as individuals need to be real.

Doing it to each other

And we're doing it to each other. There's no squiggly virus from nature or laser guided manipulation from outer space; all of this happens because we are maneuvering and manipulating each other. And our selves. ssshhh, don't tell anybody.

Many avenues are used

I am going to list several and I could fill the whole book with examples of how we are led one way when we would be better off going another. Sometimes subtly, sometimes not so subtly. It may seem innocuous when merchants raise prices on consumer goods so that they can then be discounted rather than having real discounts. I know two jewelry stores in the local mall who have had 50% discount sales on for the last 10 years. And I know people who believe that the discounts are real. They believe that the regular price is twice as much as the "sale" price. It seems small and rather insignificant lying about how much something costs but it sets the tone, it creates a script in our brains that will play endlessly. On the bright side, it is a script that can be erased.

We humans are big on consistency

We often prefer consistently bad treatment to treatment that is good, especially if the good treatment is unreliable. The "devil you know," so to speak. I have a friend who is in a bad relationship with an active alcoholic. She got fed up with his drinking and opted out of the relationship for a while and even took up with someone else. But when some decisions had to be made to define the new relationship, how they would resolve conflicts, who would take responsibility for what, she bailed out. When explaining to me why she went back to the old relationship, she explained it well.

"He's always there for me. I can depend on him"

He mooches off of her and reduces her self-esteem by berating her on an ongoing basis. Ongoing basis is the key. He is consistent. We like things to stay the same once a precedent is set. Isn't it amazing how we get into these traps and stay there forever unless we break out.

The number of commercials keep sneaking up on us gradually so they seem to stay consistent and they are consistently bad, at least most of them. We love to hate them, complain about them, and consistently watch them. Most people believe that most commercials are dishonest and that wrestling is phoney. But since they are accepted, the precedents have been set, we have consciously or unconsciously made a commitment to watch them any way. We are set up for ever increasing amounts of mindless drivel punctuated by violence.

Consistency in the showroom

Car salesmen have been loading many of us up with deluxe entertainment systems, specially treated leather interiors, special paint jobs, and assorted other goodies because we are vulnerable after signing the contract for a new car. They have been doing it for years and we make jokes about it. It's the way it is, we accept it because we want things to be consistent and then joke about it to take the edge off. So it ends up that we make a commitment to buy the car and naturally, to remain consistent, we buy the extras especially since they seem so inexpensive (in relation to the big ticket car price). "It really was the right decision to buy the car and to prove it, I am going to buy some more. Yes, we would like the car company's credit card, we'll be coming here for service anyway. Yes, we'll take the extra warranty, then we won't have to worry about anything."

"Oh, you have insurance too?"

"Well my goodness, how convenient. Well it is a little expensive and that credit card sure does have a high interest rate but this way I can keep everything together and that counts for something. And the credit card has discounts for motel accommodations as well as death benefits."

It counts for a lot of money, from you to the car dealer who has his business on a one way street. Not that the customer gets nothing, the customer gets all of the products he pays for but the extra benefits that "compliance tacticians" accumulate all flow in one direction. Isn't it interesting how making additional commitments (after making the first one) is just a matter of being consistent. The process in this book can be used for deciding if you should buy a new car, and if you decide to, it can be used during the process of buying it. To do what is best for you rather than the car dealer.

A beautiful place

The bad part for me is that we are at such a beautiful place in our evolution. A psychologist in California discovered that he could teach his daughter to read while he was teaching her to talk; by the age of two. Think what a giant step it would be for us if all kids could learn to speak and read by the age of two and really become excellent speakers and readers by the age of four. That's when the language window in the brain begins to narrow. We also have the opportunity to teach them how to make decisions and value judgements by the time they go to kindergarten. Instead, we let the television program our kids far too much (and far too often); program them for violence. Violence begets violence. Passive, mindless behavior in front of a television set promotes mindless, passive behavior in front of a television set; and violence.

Discoveries being ignored

It seems ironic to me that our DNA, the storehouse for information, the collection of ancient memories and designs for the future is being ignored by everyday people. There is so much being discovered about how we operate as humans, not only DNA but other disciplines as well, that can be used to better our lives. We have instant access to other parts of the world via television and the internet. Information about how the mind works is exploding and is available in books, classrooms, the internet, computer software, television, and many other forums. There is a tremendous amount of information about how we can be more successful. Much of it is over 20 years old and is being ignored. Much of it is brand new and being ignored.

It is such a shame that much of our nation is opting for mindless activities. The politicians are playing "gotcha." We are a nation in decline and it will continue unless we do something about it. The education that our children get today does not compete well on the world market. Tomorrow our country will not compete well on the world market. These conditions exist at our peril. This makes it imperative for each of us to focus on self improvement. To clear away the maya. We need to become better parents, better citizens, better at our professions; better to ourselves and our country. The human species has developed to where we can be Self-Evolutionary in the context of the whole human race as well as ourselves individually.

I present this book

So it is in this environment that I present this book containing a process for becoming much more thoughtful and successful. It's a rational process based partly on the way that we evolved a step at a time; a thought at a time. The process uses Self-Evolutionary templates, guides that you fill information into (in a logical, thoughtful, manner) that then directs your brain in the direction "you want to go in." You can now create your own subjective reality, your vision, and project it out into the future in a compelling manner. You can use your vision to clear away the disinformation and get right to the heart of the matter: "you were born to be successful in all areas of your life and hundreds if not thousands of people have been trying to talk you out of it." The often misguided and very often disastrous disinformation comes from many quarters. On a Sunday in June, 1945, Father Freeze, the Catholic priest of our local parish told me (and everybody else) in a sermon in St. Joseph's Church that unless I suffered as Jesus Christ suffered on the cross, I would not get to heaven, indeed I would go to hell. I was almost 5 and understood what he said well enough to decide to injure myself, for as long as necessary, to avoid hell. That hell is over for me and I have moved on but I still find a lot of disinformation, a lot of maya to sort through.

I wrote this book for me, I need it.

If I pay too much attention to what is going on externally, I sometimes become defocused and even depressed; anxious. I have to go inside and find a positive point of view. Thinking has gone out of style and thinking is what we are designed to do. We need cogent thought processes to direct our brains and enjoy the "times that we live in." The assaults on our senses are chipping away at the structure in our life: the family, productivity in the nation, our education system, the fabric of our culture. We are the most violent nation on the face of the earth. We are not developing the potential of our country or ourselves as we should. In many ways we are going backward.

We know more about our thinking than we ever have and we are learning more all of the time. Thinking could even become fashionable again. Wouldn't that be something. A renaissance in thinking; making decisions; qualifying and enhancing beliefs; predicting the consequence of our actions; projecting our visions into the future; turning feedback into success: this could be the beginning of a new era, a renaissance in cognition. It is to that end that this book is dedicated. Good luck with your adventures using the Self-Evolutionary process. I hope you will be as successful as you want to be.

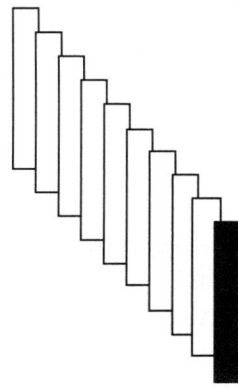

Look Forward

set (set) v. set,setting,sets. -tr. **13**. To prescribe or to establish.

The American Heritage Dictionary

Would you like to be SET for Success? Would you like to schedule yourself for prosperity. Would you like to take a walk in your mind and explore *your* reality for success.

David A. Jacobi

What is Your Reality?

What is actual, what is true? Are you ready to pursue *your* reality; to look for the process that brings you success; to find the steps that you can take to reach your goals; using your capabilities; within your "frame of reference?" Look for my picture as you read the book. I'll make some points for you to consider. You can make it an adventure as you explore thought processes in the rarely examined, sometimes nebulous parts of your gray matter. Let's take a walk in your mind and get a glimpse of how you organize your thoughts and your life. Let's find out what points you in the right direction and gives you traction to move forward.

Life can be more than becoming the manager of the department or buying a new truck; writing a play or becoming a better parent (all worthy endeavors). Life can also be finding out what makes us stand up straight. Finding out if there are spiritual principles worth dying for. What do we value the most, our lives, our families, or certain principles and should we ever have to choose between them? What are our hidden capabilities, and how do we evaluate our attitudes?

You can establish some of the ways that we use time and space. Time and space are big elements in our expanding universe so we have a lot to create from; how do we divide time and space into steps around a dance floor, into thoughts about the past, or raising a child. How can we write, direct, and produce movies in our minds of what we want to become. Would you like to find out? You can learn to use your brain with great facility, elegantly, and see the Northern Lights.

Is reality something that you search for in books, in lectures, in conversation with your neighbor, or is it something that you create in your mind? Maybe it's is all of those things and more. Should you be a dreamer like Einstein, or a realist like Churchill, or both? Can powerful mental techniques override emotional scars deep in the psyche? Can belief move mountains? Should success be achieved in a spectacular accomplishment or is it best achieved in incremental, sure-footed steps? Can the steps for success fit into a template?

Maybe the things that we are unsuccessful at are things that we just haven't learned how to do yet, or do we sometimes sabotage ourselves? I recently read that "most" lottery winners are worse off financially, after a couple of years, than before they won the money. Is believing that you deserve success more important than the thoughts and actions that you use to arrive at your goal? Life is a challenge and always will be. Part of that challenge is self-discovery; finding out what symbols, images, ideas, concepts, and character types you recall from your memory when planning and accomplishing tasks. And probably more important are the new ways of thinking and doing.

The question for me is how to meet life on "its terms," become more successful, develop an attitude for success, and then look for new challenges because they are exciting. What is reality for you?

Maybe the best solution is for everyone to write their own book on how to succeed, and in a sense, that is what this book is about. We each have our belief systems containing what we believe works in life, what is of value to us, what we are willing to work for; this book asks you to take a look at success from your perspective and then put it into a Self-Evolutionary template. The process in this book asks you to create subjective reality, your ideas for success, put them into a particular sequence, that's what the template is for, so that you can then act them out intelligently and thoughtfully. But I hope I am also provocative; that I provoke critical and creative thinking so that you can be flexible enough in your search for reality to come up with what is right for you.

> What will it take to make you more successful?

My Responsibility

It is my responsibility to articulate the dynamic process I have developed and present it to you in this book, in the best way that I know how. But nothing works for everyone. If this model doesn't work for you, you have tried and I have tried and the experience is a lesson in itself. There are no guarantees in life and I make no guarantee that this process will work for everyone. I do, however, believe strongly that it will be valuable for everyone industrious enough to give it a fair trial. I also realize that I will be asking some of you to think about and perform certain mental gymnastics that you have never performed. If you are **not** neurologically impaired, you can do them. Give yourself some time when necessary. Give yourself permission.

Your Responsibility

It is up to you to read and believe or disbelieve. It's up to you to use the process, design your own templates, or throw the book out. It is also your responsibility to go to a qualified mental health professional (or some other resource) if you have emotional or mental problems. While success is good for you physically, mentally, emotionally, and spiritually, this book is **not** designed to alleviate problems if you are sabotaging yourself (although it may).

If you have emotional problems and you would like to use this book as an adjunct to therapy, talk to your mental health professional. It seems like a great idea to me. If someone doesn't feel they deserve success they create resistance to success. The more powerful a process is the more resistance will be generated. If, when you use this process, you try to go in one direction but keep ending up in the opposite direction, or if success makes you stressed or unhappy, it's a good idea to look into some counselling. You'll have a lot to talk about with the resource that you choose.

Success or Failure

Some years ago I read a book by Maxwell Maltz called *Psycho-Cybernetics*.[1] I believed then and I believe now that the brain uses "cybernetic like" functions to accomplish what we **want** in life. When we *error* (when we program ourselves *incorrectly)* we get what we **don't** want in life. In the cybernetic model, feedback is an important control mechanism for our thought processes and can be used in what Maltz called a "goal-striving mechanism." It's up to us to program ourselves for success rather than failure and how to achieve the correct programming has been an intriguing question for a very long time. I am going to give you a very good answer.

Self Image

Maltz's book made a big issue about the self image; how we feel about ourselves; the model of ourselves that we refer to when we entertain ideas, evaluate beliefs, choose strategies, and get on with our everyday lives. I believe that success can make us feel very good about ourselves, very quickly. Success speaks very well to the unconscious. Our self image depends on a number of factors: our beliefs, values, and capabilities but also our behavior. If we say that we believe in honesty and then put a five dollar bill into the collection basket while we take change for a ten, our unconscious knows what we really are. "By their deeds you will know them" applies to self image also. Our unconscious looks at our behavior and makes judgements. If you keep performing a behavior, even if you don't believe in it, it will become accepted as part of you. This is one reason accomplishments make us feel good about ourselves and why we shouldn't do anything we are **not** comfortable with, unless we "want" to be comfortable with it.

I liked his book, read it several times, but as far as I know it never helped me and I certainly could have used the help. But I use it as a reference, now. I think that it was a book before its time in that good ideas were put forth but the techniques to transform them into behavior were *yet* to be developed. It drew a map that said you could get from here to there, but the transport, the mental machinery, was yet to be discovered.

Self Help Books

Psycho-Cybernetics is just one of many self-help books that have been published over the years with great ideas, good philosophy, and worthy objectives but far too often, **not** enough instructions on how to obtain the results. The train most often left the station with few people on board.

It might be instructive to look at two points of view about change. Please keep in mind that these are just two points of view among many and are used to gain perspective rather than to provide definitive answers. The first is from Anthony Robbins in his book *Awaken the Giant Within* and the second is from *The Right Brain and the Unconscious* by Dr. R. Joseph.

Anthony Robbins

Most people have no idea of the giant capacity we can immediately command when we focus all of our resources on mastering a single area of our lives. Controlled focus is like a laser beam that can cut through anything that seems to be stopping you... I've continued to recognize the power individuals have to change virtually anything and everything in their lives in an instant. I've learned that the resources we need to turn our dreams into reality are within us, merely waiting for the day when we decide to wake up and claim our birthright.[2]

Dr. R. Joseph

In considering the multitude of forces that act on human beings— selective pressures over the course of evolution, heredity, genetics, biochemical fluctuations, how our parents raised us, and the cultural biases that we are all subject to— it may well seem that all our behavior is determined by causal factors set in motion so long ago that

15

we are helpless to alter their course. Certainly order exists in the universe, we are affected by our environment, and forces such as fate, God, or even our astrological sign (if we wish to believe in such things) may exert some influences on our behavior. Nevertheless...We are still capable of making choices...what we think can actually change our neurochemical environment as well as the actual structure of our brain. If we think new thoughts or think old thoughts in a different way and apply different meanings and interpretations to them, we can expand and stretch the limits that our biological makeup has imposed. This process is called learning. Even a person who is mentally retarded is capable of making choices and being happy. [3]

Since we all have different views of the world I am **not** going to try and decide what you should or should **not** think about these two quotes. Rather than try to come up with a *definitive* statement of the human condition, I would like to summarize the two books, briefly, and then ask some questions; as a way of probing our minds.

Anthony Robbin's book is very positive. It's an excellent book and has a broad scope. Is his book more positive, more realistic than Dr. Joseph's: how does one tell? Anthony treats blocks to success as things to be removed quickly and easily. I would prefer the information be contained in more than one book and the instructions to be more detailed, more specific. This is a book to be studied and used over a period of time.

Dr. Joseph's book is **not** a self help book in the usual sense. Is his book more realistic? It's an excellent book and gives a good account of how our evolution and conditioning determine a lot of our present day characteristics. He gives a comprehensive look at the usual brain-mind topics including our unconscious, the two hemispheres of the brain (lateralization), and how we can remember the past and contemplate the future. He explains in detail how the circuits in our brains were formed in childhood and why we are often self-defeating in business, relationships, health, etc. Dr. Joseph is an internationally recognized theorist and neuroscientist, an expert on both the mind and brain; he is also a psychotherapist and neuropsychologist.

This Book

The process described in this book is an evolutionary process in that it looks at the mental processes we developed as we became bipedal, learned to speak one word after another, to perform mathematics in steps, and write computer code a line at a time. A temporal-sequential process is where we do things a step at a time. I have taken the components for success, put them into a temporal-sequential order, a very natural order, and then describe techniques that you can use to design and implement a successful experience. It's also an adventure where you find out what the reality of success is, for you.

This book describes a generic process that is "relatively" simple once you learn to use it. It can be used over and over again for creating change within yourself and for accomplishing tasks in your everyday life. You can use it to help recover from a stroke, become drug and alcohol free, overcome eating disorders, buy a house, or change your attitude toward your neighbor; if you choose to. If you have had an accident and you need determination and a positive "mind set" to walk again, this book shows you how to get your supply of resolve from within. Because of the generic nature of this process, ideas from other books can be incorporated in the strategy component of the Self-Evolutionary process. Blocks to success *may* be overcome in the process of using this book but I leave therapy to mental health professionals.

Beliefs, Decisions, and Strategies

Beliefs, decisions, and strategies are very interesting to me. For instance, did President Truman **believe** he had to stop the Soviet Union from taking over West Berlin in 1948 first, and then make the **decision** to defend it second? I think he did. The **strategy** of an airlift came later and although many initially thought it would **not** work, it was a monumental achievement, a great success. President Truman is known to have been a decision maker and is now highly regarded. But with the atomic bomb, he had the **strategy** of using it before he had to make the **decision** to bomb Japan. His decision to use it was largely based on the **belief** that it would save lives. So did he have a **strategy** first, then a **belief**, and then the **decision**? These three components of success have a very interesting relationship.

Self-Evolutionary Templates

I've taken my knowledge and experience in life, common sense, and psychology into the workshop of my mind and evolved what I am calling Self-Evolutionary templates and thus the name of the book. A Self-Evolutionary template is a container where you insert your ideas for success. The template provides a logical sequence for your ideas (your vision) and helps you embed them into your unconscious in a compelling manner. You then have a conscious and an unconscious plan of action that you can use to perform the tasks required to obtain your goal.

The Self-Evolutionary Process

This process is self-evolutionary in the sense that as members of the human race we have our own personal evolutions. The human mind has evolved to the point that we can now use it, to a very large degree, to direct our own personal growth. It's self-evolutionary in the "cybernetic" sense that we not only think, but can also observe, get feedback from, modify, and enhance thinking, so that we can design processes that make us become more capable. Professional golfers may develop a waggle when in front of the ball to feel their way into a state of excellence. They may go through specific thought processes to pull up memories and feelings of when they were "in the zone" before in order to be successful once again. Every shot, every green, every tournament provides feedback.

This process is self-evolutionary in the sense that the more we evolve, the more we *can*. You can use this process to model the way that your boss conducts business and then use that model when you go into business for yourself. If the model is good enough, you can write a book about it and pass it along to others. You would then have evolved and become a business person-author. When successful at one business you could go into a number of businesses and when wealthy, you could become a business person-author-philanthropist. The concept of always refining and getting better is inherit in the human condition.

A Generic Process

This process is generic. It has more to do with form than

content. Specific content is added to the process to accomplish a specific task but the process itself is general enough so that it can accommodate a wide variety of tasks. Tasks can be looked at individually or as building blocks in a hierarchy of improvement. Much the way reading, writing, and speaking can be improved if you want to become a professional communicator. The way that changing diet and getting more exercise can lead to better health which can lead to a more productive and fulfilling life. A more fulfilling life can change beliefs and values which can then lead to identity changes and new spiritual directions.

Thoughts About Change

The basic premise of this book is that we have evolved to the point where we can be a lot more responsible for our own evolution. The "other primates" are unable to do this. Some believe that we have special responsibilities because of the special way that we have evolved. Some of us want to get at the very essence of life while others want to just enjoy the rapture of it. I would like you to go in the direction that you want to go in; for as long as you want to.

How to Use This Book

Read the Summary in the back of the book on page 161 first.

- Part One of this book establishes the foundation for the Self-Evolutionary process. It's technical in some parts as it explains how we evolved and why we think the way we do. It explains the underpinnings of the process and is very important. You will be referred to the Appendix for some of the more detailed descriptions of brain function.

- Part Two begins with an overview and then gives step-by-step instructions for designing and implementing a Self-Evolutionary template to obtain a goal.

- Some of us want to "do" things and have little patience for explanations. If you learn best by doing, you may want to read Part Two first and learn how to use the process to obtain a goal right away. I recommend that you use the process for something of less importance the first time and then read the complete book, the sooner the better.

Thoughts are Valuable

Robert B. Cialdini writes in his book, *Influence, The Psychology of Persuasion*[4] that "After eons of slow accumulation human knowledge has snowballed into an era of momentum-fed, multiplicative, monstrous expansion." He goes on to say that most of the information we have today is less than 15 years old. In some fields, some people believe that knowledge doubles every eight years. This produces a competitive environment where our time, energy, and successful thoughts become very valuable.

Look to the Future

And look at what new developments await us in the future. Imagine commanding one of the walls of your home to call your brother or sister. As the call is placed, the whole wall becomes an electronic, holographic screen that opens up into your brother or sisters living room. You talk to your brother or sister's family in full size, three dimensional, high definition, stereophonic sound. Let's say that you read two books on abstract art the night before and the internet described a Willem deKooning exhibition at the Metropolitan Museum. Both families share the museum experience together, via the internet, in virtual reality, and after going through and viewing all of deKooning's works that interest you, you send a multi-media tape of the complete experience, via e-mail, to a brother or sister who was backpacking in the Rocky Mountains and didn't have time to make the trip; so they make it with you, later.

Endnotes

1. M. Maltz, *Psycho-Cybernetics* (No. Hollywood: Wilshire Book Company, 1960).

2. A. Robbins, *Awaken the Giant Within* (New York: Fireside, 1991).

3. R. Joseph, *The Right Brain and the Unconscious* (New York: Plenum Press, 1992).

4. R. B. Cialdini *Influence: The Psychology of Persuasion* (New York: William and Morrow, 1993).

Part One

Part One is the basis for Part Two where Self-Evolutionary templates are designed and implemented (installed in your conscious and unconscious awareness).

Part One describes how the mind evolved as our ancestors scratched, fought, and thought their way to survival and prosperity. It depicts how the brain flashes images, provides floods of feelings, and creates logic in our internal dialogue.

Part One provides the mental tools used for creating the Self-Evolutionary templates.

With time and experience, the Self-Evolutionary process will help you develop a successful personality.

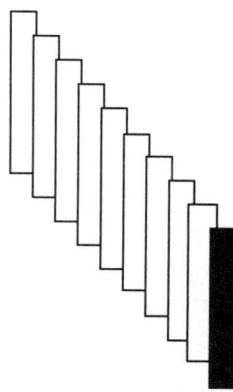

Preview of the Process

Since Part One provides the mental tools used for creating
Self-Evolutionary templates, let's preview the Self-
Evolutionary process to get an understanding of how the
mental tools might be applied. How does the way we evolved
and how our brains function apply to the Self-Evolutionary
process?

The Self-Evolutionary Process

1. **Entertain Ideas**. We have thousands of thoughts each day,
   some are important enough to act on. It's often helpful to know
   where ideas come from when using the Self-Evolutionary
   process. If certain problems keep coming from a common
   source, you may want to look at the source; maybe something
   can be done to stop things from happening in the first place.

2. **Qualify an Idea**. This is where you examine the idea that you want to pursue and ensure that it is a good one. You look at what happens if you obtain your goal, what happens if you don't.

3. **Believe**. This is where you "empower" the belief that you are going to be successful in obtaining your goal. This is where you use subjective experience, all five senses plus language to empower that belief.

4. **Decide**. This is where you compare alternative options to be sure that your goal is the best one available. It is a brain storming session and a decision process. When you are sure that you have the very best goal, you use your subjective experience, all five senses plus language, to make a firm commitment.

5. **Choose a Strategy**. This is where you choose the strategy that will take you to your goal. This component, like Decide, is a brain storming session and a decision process, and like the other components, uses the five senses plus language.

6. **Project the Outcome**. This is where you project your goal into the future by; image, feeling, and sound (smell and taste per your appetite). This is where you project your vision into the future using your mental tools. The more compelling you project it, the better chance for success.

7. **Project the Effects**. This is where you project the effects of your goal into the future, in the appropriate time frame, by image, feeling, and sound (smell and taste per your appetite). The effects are usually more long term than the goal that produced them and make the directions to your brain more complete, more comprehensive.

8. **Perform Rehearsal**. This is where you create and preview a powerful mental state (whether it be excitement, focus, joy, relaxation, or a combination of states) that you will be in when you perform the task needed to obtain your goal.

9. **Analyze the Results**. Analyze the results of the performance to see how it can be made better.

A reference component can be used to enhance subjective experience. A weak belief can be turned into a strong belief, for instance. Most of the components can be made more powerful using the mental tools from the Mental Tools chapter.

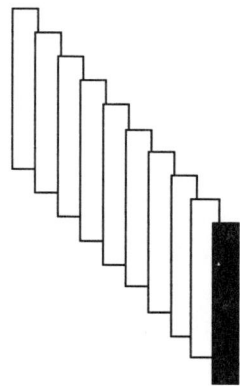

Look Backward

Our ancestors became bipedal, walked out of Africa, and peopled the rest of the world. They expanded both sides of their brains; learned to speak and think using language; developed art and science; the social, political, and cultural complexities that we call civilization; it took 5 to 10 million years to do it. Using upright locomotion gave our ancestors great advantage in their evolution. The thinking that evolved has made us what we are. What then is the connection between upright locomotion, language, thinking, and success for you?

Look to the Past

To help us understand how our thought processes "guide us" now and predict how they will "guide us" in the future, it's helpful to see where they came from. Flashes of insight, trial and error developed the mental tools that we use to design and implement goals. They evolved as we became bipedal, sailed the oceans, and inhabited all continents on earth. If Cro-Magnon people could project ideas into the future, we can too. For those of you who want to become self-evolutionary and to chart your own course into the future, feel free to think ahead and to speculate on your own. And, since we are going back in time, we might as well go back to the beginning.

The Universe

As near, or as far as we can tell, the universe exploded and is still exploding at the speed of light. It's been doing so for 10 to 20 billion years. Its interesting that this was, as far as we know, a one-time event. Most things in our universe have a frequency. The atoms in my hand and the light coming from the computer screen are all reoccurring and thus have a rate of repetition, a frequency. If the big bang has a frequency, it's a very long time between beats. Most of the universe is cold and dark but very fast. Some of the universe is very hot, hydrogen-bomb-bursting hot. It started with a big bang and is still banging; most astronomers believe. I don't know if it is or not. **It sure is stable**. The same speed, the speed of light for 10, 15, or 20 billion years? That's the kind of stability you can depend on, *for a long time.*

The Big Bang

The big bang started everything but was there something here before the big bang? Did a grain of sand explode? Or did the forerunner of this universe collapse and then reverse itself on the other side like a sock being turned inside out. Some astronomers believe that this is what is going to happen to our universe, it will implode on itself, and what if it did? Would we notice the difference? Experiments have shown that our eyes can adjust to seeing everything in reverse with special mirrored glasses; after a time, it becomes normal.

We can turn our awareness inside out. That's pretty amazing when you think about it but then we have had an amazing evolution, haven't we? But instead of turning our mind inside out we developed two of them, one in the left hemisphere and the other in the right hemisphere. They form a parallel processing super computer.

And where did we come from? Every atom in each of our bodies came from the stars. Is that why we look at them in amazement and awe? Is the universe part of us?

Was space here before the universe was created and what is space? If I decide that space is something, an expanse, a stretch of something, anything at all, then I come to the conclusion that the universe always was. *Always was* is real stability. And always will be? The sun is good for another 5 to 10 billion years and my guess is that there is time to make other arrangements. Maybe there is a planet in the milky way that has the weather of California, no earthquakes, and the air quality of Iceland; nothing down, self-evolutionists welcome.

The Solar System

The sun and planets, as near or as far as we can tell, began as interstellar dust out toward the edge of our galaxy which we call the Milky Way. (Snicker, Snicker.) Somehow, something got it all started: it began rotating, developed gravity, the center got bigger and faster and hotter until at some point, after millions of years, the core ignited and became a continually exploding thermonuclear reaction; we call it our sun. It's a relatively small, yellow star. The nearest star to our star (the sun) is about 25 trillion miles away. When our solar system was created, instead of a big bang, things just seemed to swirl together. There are many types of activities in the universe.

Planets formed from the debris that was left over. The debris was swirling around: planetoids, asteroids, comets, dirt, and ice bumping into itself, continually rearranging, until it began to coalesce into separate units. The separate units are now rotating around the sun, in a very precise manner. This good earth is one of them.

The Earth

The third planet from the sun, the dwelling place of humankind, is a sphere that was created around four and a half billion years ago. It was created when the rest of the solar system swirled into existence, and in pretty much the same manner. It sunbathes all year, clouds permitting, rolling over once every 23 hours and 56.07 minutes. The earth turns on its axis as it rotates around the sun. All of the planets rotate around the sun, but differently. While the planets rotate around the sun, the sun has its own orbit in the Milky Way, and the Milky Way has its own orbit, **way, way, out there**.

Humankind

My guess is that our ancestors looked at the universe in wonderment and fear. They probably looked at the stars in wonderment. I do. On a clear night, in the country (away from the pollution), with friends or alone, the night sky is still one of the best shows on the planet. It's a beautiful way to let your awareness expand and increase as you move among the stellar luminaries.

The sun must have been viewed as a friend. It melted the fear of night, provided warmth, furnished a way to judge time, gave light to travel and hunt by, and caused the fast drying of animal skins. The setting of the sun must have caused trepidation. But then, dark nights and wild animals must also have given our ancestors something to look forward to and looking forward to morning surely instilled in them the ability to project into the future. Something did.

I am sure that our ancestors feared the flashing spears of lightning and the earth shaking blows of thunder. "Why is the earth so angry?" I wonder about that some times, myself. Watching an intense thunderstorm where lightning rips the air apart and thunder slams it back together excites me somewhere in that early part of my existence. And what a relief as the thunder and lightning becomes more distant and the earth becomes comfortable again; when our friend the sun comes back to keep us warm and comfortable.

Our ancestors looked at the universe they lived in and learned to meet the challenges of life; to grow and prosper. But how did they do it? What was their reality?

Bipedalism

The African continent is being torn apart by tectonic plates deep within; about an inch a year and has been for about 30 million years. Richard Leakey in *Origins Reconsidered* explains what the east part of Africa was like 5 to 10 million years ago:

> As a result of the separation of tectonic plates running roughly north-south underneath the eastern part of the continent, upwelling lava gradually caused the crust to bulge unevenly, building the Kenyan dome and the Ethiopian dome, each reaching about nine thousand feet above sea level. Like huge blisters on the continental skin, these two domes brought large-scale topography to East Africa. At the time, a swath of dense rain forest stretched across the continent, from the Atlantic coast to the Indian

Ocean, home to an increasing diversity of ape species. As the two great domes grew, the patterns of rainfall to the east were disrupted, the result of a growing rain shadow. The eastern forests began to fragment, and patches of open country developed, producing a mosaic of environments, from forest to woodland to shrub and grassland.[1]

The Great Rift Valley that dipped and spread the earth open, sometimes deep and sometimes shallow, sometimes arid and sometimes moist, stretched for about three thousand miles from the Red Sea to present day Mozambique. In the process it provided a multitude of microenvironments, a diversity of species, and because of inherent instability, a hot house for evolutionary change. I used to love to talk about the Great Rift Valley causing great savannas and how our ancestors stood up to see over the tall grass and became bipedal. Probably not, but it was a good story.

What Happened

What probably happened is that a cooling climate from an ice age was added to the instable environment causing the ape species to be challenged, many became extinct; one species however, became bipedal because it had to go greater distances for food. Food is such an immediate and primary need that it could very well have made the difference. I suspect that there were a lot of contributing factors that caused our ancestors to walk on two feet.

Some contend that our ancestors became bipedal in order to carry things. For the male, being able to bring food back to the female, who had developed a continuous sex drive, was an advantage. The female was then able to have more offspring and thus grow the race. It's more likely that females provided most of the food by hunting small animals and gathering nuts, berries, fruits, greens, and roots.

Of course, standing up allowed the evolving species to see farther, navigate the terrain better, and have better warning when enemies approached. It's important to get a "fight or flight" strategy started early. There were many advantages to walking erect and the proof is that our ancestors survived, evolved, and prospered; like no other primate.

One Foot after Another

Our nervous system developed differently being a walker on two feet. Now that we know the stomach has a brain of its own and that it's in some ways comparable to the brain in the skull and that the whole nervous system is systemic, it seems that a vertical species would have to develop differently. Being vertical for running, walking, and standing around gives a completely different perspective; more aware of the physical environment; better able to see relationships between the physical environment, people, and prey; facing life head-on instead of looking at the ground most of the time. What is of special interest to me is that our ancestors put one foot after another (for 5 to 10 million years). Putting one foot after another can be called a "temporal-sequential activity." Putting one word after another is also a temporal-sequential activity. Maybe there's a connection.

> "One thing follows another" is a fairly simple concept, one that many animals can master. Indeed, its what most learning is all about; for Pavlov's dogs, it was bell tends to be followed by food...Acquiring vocabulary and understanding basic word order are...relatively easy language tasks for both humans and bonobos.[2]

Not that we could speak 5 to 10 million years ago. Maybe grunts, gestures, facial expressions, body posture and mimicry of animals, much like other primates, but not language. We were just a bipedal ape (one that walked on two legs) that became known as a hominid, a species that was on a very long trek that would reach the moon with an eye on the planets.

I agree with Richard Leakey and many others that bipedalism is the single most important *step* in human evolution. I suspect that temporal-sequential programming in our brains (one word follows another, one thought follows another) is the second most important. I also think that the thinking needed to perform count downs for the Apollo space program could **not** have been achieved by a species walking on four legs; or could it?

Homo Erectus

The lineage from the first bipedal hominid, fresh out of the rain forest to modern humans who surf the internet, is not established well enough for most anthropologists. But there is hope among most that the details will be filled in with fossils, DNA, and new technology. There is enough information to come to certain conclusions about the relationship between the five senses and language as it applies to becoming more successful. These conclusions are explained at different places in the book and there is also that thing about doing things a step at a time.

Homo erectus who came on the scene about 1.6 million years ago is very interesting for several reasons. Richard Leakey states that:

> *Homo erectus* stands at a pivotal point in human evolutionary history, in a very real way it is the harbinger of humanity. Everything earlier than *Homo erectus* was more apelike (except the short-lived, somewhat enigmatic *Homo habilis*). Everything after *Homo erectus* was distinctly humanlike, in behavior as well as form. The beginnings of a hunting-and-gathering way of life came with *Homo erectus*, stone tools for the first time gave the impression of standardization, the imposition of a mental template, fire was harnessed for the first time, for the first time hominids expanded beyond the African continent. And surely the rudiments of language— perhaps even consciousness—were produced in a dramatically expanding brain. [3]

Temporal-Sequential Activities

Temporal-sequential activities where we do things a step at a time show up in several places in the quote shown above.

1. Stone tool making required the flint to be flaked in a precise sequence under exacting conditions. Modern humans, after a lot of trial and error, have only recently "reacquired" the skill.

2. Fire making also required a precise set of steps. First to find combustible material, get it ignited with enough friction, nurture it to get it going, build it to a suitable flame, and then maintain it, at times even transporting it to new locations. It seems simple but we are the only primate that developed the ability.

3. Even rudimentary language requires words to follow each other.

Temporal-sequential activities were an important part of our evolution. One could wonder, even argue which came first, temporal-sequential activities or language. I think temporal-sequential activities came first and provided the mental machinery for both sophisticated tool making, language, and many other human activities. I even think that walking, putting one foot after another was the precursor for all such activities.

My imagination brings up pictures of cave parents teaching their kids to walk, to grunt, to gesture, and a plethora of body language to communicate their desires. The grunts and gestures became more sophisticated to meet the needs of a more sophisticated hunter/gatherer society. Leaders could probably maintain their authority by gestures, grunts, and body language but when it came time to plan a hunt, language was essential.

The women picking berries and roots while the men were obtaining fresh meat needed a spoken language because they were using their hands a lot. It's possible but inconvenient to hold a baby with one hand and to communicate with the other. Women were the most responsible for developing spoken language and that's probably why little girls learn to speak first as babies.

If our brains love to do things in a temporal-sequential manner, (indeed doing one thing after another has been a big part of our evolution), then temporal-sequential activities in a process designed to elicit success seems like a good approach. And if not a temporal-sequential manner, how else could we do it?

Modern Humans

The evolution of modern humans with spoken language, conscious awareness, a giant curiosity, and maybe even a hint of morality (beginning in Africa about 150,000-100,000 years ago) is difficult to establish precisely. This seems ironic since *modern* human evolution happened "recently." This is true but it is also true that we have evolved so suddenly (relatively speaking) and the fossil record is so incomplete that causal factors become confusing. It's evident that social groups became larger, they began to trade, toolmaking became more sophisticated, society became more complex, and enough self awareness and death awareness developed to bury the dead (with flowers). All of this doesn't evolve without a well developed spoken language. The ability to visualize, feel, and hear subjective experience and then project it into the future was also needed. We needed both language and the five senses which developed a special relationship.

We Have Arrived

What ever the precise origins we now have a wealth of spoken, written, sign, and computer languages with great art, great literature, and a very broad spectrum of peoples with their social and cultural trappings. Technology is exploding at an expediential rate with many different modes of communication. For instance, computer language now creates spoken, written, visual, and sound information and then promulgates it over the internet, worldwide, in seconds. For the first time in history a company's image as well as its business can be economically communicated to its employees, business partners, and customers, at the same time, all over this good earth. Individuals can have the same impact as companies on the internet. So where's the fog, you may ask?

Language and Senses

How did we learn to create image, sound, feeling, smell, and taste information in our fantasies; how did we learn to compose movies with dialogue and sound in the projection room of our brain? Richard Leakey speaks of the Loom of Language:

> When we contemplate our origins, we quickly come to focus on language. Objective standards for our uniqueness as a species, such as our bipedality and our relatively enormous brain, are easy to measure. But in many ways it is language that makes us feel human. Ours is a world of words. Our thoughts, our world of imagination, our communication, our richly fashioned culture—all are woven on the loom of language. Language can conjure up images in our minds. Language can stir our emotions— sadness, happiness, love, hatred. Through language we can express individuality or demand collective loyalty. Quite simply, language is our medium.[4]

I agree with Mr. Leakey about the importance of language, we do think linguistically for the most part but I feel that all of the five senses are important. Let's get technical just for a moment to see how language and the five senses fit together. Language is unique, it has an important place in our lives, there's nothing else quite like it; grunts, gestures, and body language have limited communication, much too limited for Shakespeare in the park or an Apollo countdown.

Language is sensory based; we use language visually as we

read, we hear it as we listen to ourselves or others speak, and we can feel it as braille. We can also feel loud music vibrate our bodies and ears, we can see the lips moving as others speak, and we can feel our mouths, lips, throat, and vocal cords as we talk.

But language is unique in that we can describe all of the five senses using language. On the other hand, without the five senses there would be no language. Or we might say that language is generated *on the loom* of the five senses. What a remarkable relationship between language and the five senses. This relationship is very powerful and essential for creating the subjective experience we use to fill Self-Evolutionary templates for success. Let's briefly list the five senses:

- Visual (images) -- we see internal images (memory and imagination) and external images (outside events). We can remember images from the past and we can create new ones; still shots or movies.

- Auditory (sounds and language) -- we hear internal sounds (memory and imagination) and external sounds (outside events). We can remember sounds from the past and we can create new ones, including dialogue; to go with our images.

- Feeling -- we have both tactile (a pinch) and emotional (the pain of loss).

- Olfactory. Smells have become less important in human evolution but are still useful.

- Gustatory. Tastes too have become less important in human evolution but are still useful.

We have a lot of mind stuff to create subjective experience with. Let's see how the five senses and language developed.

Language Development

Mr. Leakey looks at language from two points of view.

First, from a point of view of continuity— where did language evolve from. This is how scientists think because they like to get at the very essence of things. Did we inherit the cognitive abilities for language from apes or is it a uniquely human experience. His conclusion, as I interpret it, is that we inherited and then enhanced skills that were rooted in ape brains. I see grunts, gestures, and body language as the beginning point with Leo Tolstoy and Tennessee Williams as natural extensions with millions of years of trial and error in between. Although voice inflection and word order are still being experimented with, I think that mimicking the sounds of nature was important in forming new words. I wonder what the word for "burbling brook" was in early hominid? How about the words for lightning and thunder, rain and snow?

Secondly, did language evolve as a tool so that we could communicate better or was there another reason with language as a by-product?

Brain Size

Richard Leakey has studied the work of Harry Jerison of the University of California at Los Angeles who has studied brain evolution in the animal kingdom and in humans. Richard Leakey speaking of Harry Jerison's work:

> He concludes that...greater language skills resulted from our need to build mental models in our heads, not primarily as a means of better communication.[5]

Our perspectives of the world are created by the entire nervous system rather than just the part of the brain dedicated to language. We absorb information from the world using all five senses and then calculate the appropriate responses in our behavior. We can respond with physical action, loud screeching sounds, dirty looks, body posture, gestures; and with language.

Model of the World

We use all five senses plus language to live our lives. The five senses provided important clues to our ancestors for survival: the sounds of nature provided clues for enemy presence as well as wild animals; visual images for tracking game; the feel of the breeze to get down wind from game animals; the ability to look, smell, and taste to determine edible plants. This type of information was combined with language to plan and execute hunting strategies. The command to form a circle around a large animal, for instance.

We have developed complex social interactions as we fulfill social contracts; develop and share technology and information; watch and listen to opera; go to movies; create, develop, and control economic systems in what we have come to know as "civilization." We have gone to the moon and will go to Mars, politics permitting. We will use lots of temporal-sequential activities, lots of language, all five senses, and that part of our brains that we can't see directly; our unconscious. What a power house, the five senses and the ability to use language. What a power house for creating subjective experience to be installed on a Self-Evolutionary template and then used to schedule us for success.

The Process Defined

Bipedalism and temporal-sequential activities in the brain led to a metamorphosis in the lives of our ancestors producing refined toolmaking, language, and the other accoutrements of civilization. Indeed, all of civilization could be viewed as the way that we divide time and space, how we put one word after another, how we perform one mathematical operation after another, how we build houses, and how we negotiate treaties. Since we use temporal-sequential activities for most everything else, it makes sense to use them for achieving goals.

What is a Self-Evolutionary template? I described a Self-Evolutionary template earlier as: a guide that you put ideas for success into. Your visions, your feelings, and language are installed in the template, in a logical thoughtful manner. The template is then used to direct your brain toward a successful resolution.

Endnotes

1. R. Leakey *Origins Reconsidered* (New York: Doubleday, 1992).
2. W. Calvin *How Brains Think* (New York: Basic Books, 1996).
3. R. Leakey *Origins Reconsidered* (New York: Doubleday, 1992).
4. Ibid.
5. Ibid.

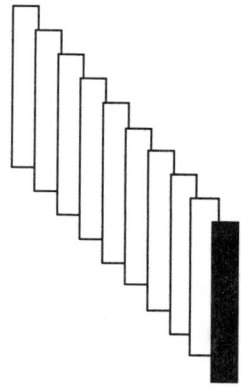

Look Inward

Consciousness is a much smaller part of our mental life than we are conscious of, because we cannot be conscious of what we are not conscious of.

Julian Jaynes

Having been blessed with bipedalism and temporal-sequential processing in our brains, having developed some constructive ways of dividing time and space, what now? What kind of thought processes do we have? How do we think, learn, and succeed; are they conscious or unconscious processes?

What is Consciousness?

The American Heritage Dictionary defines consciousness as:

1.a. having an awareness of one's own existence, sensations, and thoughts, and one's environment.

This definition is too broad for our purposes. We operate at different levels of consciousness (different levels of awareness) so let's be more specific but not too specific. There are more levels of awareness in the mind than we need to cover here.

Consciousness is simply being alive and awake.

Conscious awareness is heedful attentiveness. Being aware of a number of things that we are doing and what is happening in our environment but not all; not even most of what we are doing, seeing, hearing, and feeling. Have you ever been driving while talking to someone else in the car, or if alone thinking about family or a hobby when you suddenly discover a cop car in back of you. Where did it come from so suddenly? The cop wants to pass and you graciously move to the next lane so that he or she may, now that you are so "heedfully" attentive.

Unconscious awareness is the large number of things that we are **not** aware of, but can become aware of, like the cop car. We can become aware of our breathing, adjust it so that we are more relaxed, and after a time, become "unconsciously aware" of it again.

Unconscious: I like the American Heritage definition:

> The division of the psyche not subject to direct conscious observation but inferred from its effect on conscious processes and behavior.

I would add that although we are not capable of "conscious observation" of the unconscious we can communicate with it and influence it. Saying the ABCs in a sing-song manner as an aid to memory is one way; the whole idea of using spatial associations and a Self-Evolutionary template, both explained later, are also examples.

Conscious Awareness/Unconscious Awareness

We don't walk around aware of all of our sensations, monitoring all of our thoughts. We focus on what we are doing with the help of the reticular formation in the brain stem.

> The reticular formation plays an important role in maintaining wakefulness...It also monitors and filters the information coming in through the senses. If, for example, you are in a room with a clock that is ticking quietly, you will quickly habituate to the sound so that after a short while you will no longer hear it. But the sound is still being continually monitored by the brain, and if the clock were suddenly to stop, or to change speed or volume, you would immediately notice it. The reticular formation would have alerted you.[1]

Learning and Thinking

We have evolved in a manner that allows us to turn a lot of what we do over to automatic mechanisms in our brain and nervous system, if for no other reason; short term memory is limited. At first glance, it may seem that this could cause us to be severely limited in forming concepts, learning, and thinking; but this is not the case.

Concepts

Concepts are classes of behaviorally equivalent things or events that form general ideas or understanding. They are easily formed and easily applied, unconsciously; we do it all of the time. We can see a chair but the concept of a chair is unconscious. We might describe the "concept" of a chair as "something to sit on" and a chair usually comes to mind but we can't sit on a concept. We can describe concepts because we can assign words to represent them but the concepts themselves are unconscious.

Learning

Often conscious awareness is **not** only **not** necessary for learning but is undesirable. Learning to juggle for instance can be taught; as a matter of fact it can be learned by reading a book along with experimentation but until the "unconscious" makes the right connections you will never be able to juggle. And you have no way of knowing what the right connections are (consciously, in a straight forward manner) or you could learn them quite easily; *consciously*.

Even in a classroom where learning is assumed to be performed in a conscious fashion, most of the learning is done unconsciously. The right hemisphere of the brain reads between the lines, hears voice inflection and tempo, sees body language, and a myriad of other attributes as the unconscious makes a phenomenal number of associations with previous learning.

Word processing packages for computers are more the same than different nowadays. If you learn one, the others come easily. Any time you learn any computer application there are a tremendous number of mental links to other programs you have learned in the past, just waiting to be made. All of the links to all of the other learnings cannot be made consciously because there just isn't time and the window of consciousness is just too narrow.

The words being spoken, the words that we are consciously

aware of are in a very narrow window in short term memory. The words previously spoken a moment before are being assimilated and readied for long term memory; in an unconscious manner. An entire speech, class, event, or book has to be assimilated, categorized, synthesized, and put into memory for it to become part of our knowledge. Taking good notes in class gives the association process a second chance which provides better understanding and puts the information into a firmer place in memory. We can even memorize our notes which might be a good idea but the conscious mind is capable of seven (plus or minus two) bits of information at any given time. Most of our learning is done unconsciously.

Assimilation

Exactly how all of the information we learn in a class, in a college education, in a lifetime is integrated in our memories is still something of a mystery. But it is also magical allowing us a "spark" of creativity to redecorate the living room, a change of heart when needed to maintain a relationship, the ability to change beliefs and to make decisions for a happier life-style. The fact that we don't completely understand how we assimilate knowledge is okay. It means that we won't understand all of the electrical activity in the brain that elicits the success, and since most of what we do is done unconsciously, it doesn't matter. How we present information to the unconscious mind does matter, whether we use spatial associations and a Self-Evolutionary template or other methods.

Thinking

So if most of our learning is done unconsciously, how do we think? Mostly it's an unconscious process. Julian Jaynes described a simple experiment for making judgements way back in 1977:

> A simple experiment, so simple as to seem trivial, will bring us directly to the heart of the matter. Take any two unequal objects, such as a pen and pencil or two unequally filled glasses of water, and place them on the desk in front of you. Then, partly closing your eyes to increase your attention to the task, pick up each one with the thumb and forefinger and judge which is heavier. Now introspect on everything you are doing. You will find yourself conscious

of the feel of the objects against the skin of your fingers, conscious of the slight downward pressure as you feel the weight of each, conscious of any proturberances on the side of the objects, and so forth. And now the actual judging of which is heavier. Where is that? Lo! the very act of judgement that one object is heaver than the other is not conscious.[2]

One might feel heavier but where do we make the calculation? The feeling is in the hand but do we make the calculation in the hand or in the unconscious? Many people, when they have two objects in their hands and are looking to judge their relative weights, often move their hands up and down to help the process and indeed it probably does. I would guess that even the act of moving the hands up and down is intuitive but even if one were to think about it first, and then move the hands up and down, the calculation is unconscious. The same as when we decide that the grass needs to be mowed or we need a haircut. Unless of course we measure our grass or hair. And even then, how would we know when to measure them.

Think again at the movement of the hands when making a judgement. The two hands are connected to the two opposite hemispheres of the brain. We may be balancing the analytical, comparative, conscious left hemisphere that is capable of language with the right hemisphere that is more capable of synthesis, perception, movement, and inference but has limited language abilities. We don't use all of these capabilities to judge weight but I wonder what neural pathways are used for arriving at our view of reality?

I wonder when in our evolution we first learned to balance things with our hands? The hands must have been the first scale but I wonder who the first person was to say "well on the one hand..."

What would happen if you made decisions with your hands? You might designate one hand as yes and the other as no. Hold the hands out and ask a question. If one hand goes down will that accurately reflect what your unconscious is thinking? Maybe the first question that you ask should be whether or not this is a viable method for questioning the unconscious and making decisions.

Since we gestured before we spoke, I wonder what kind of judgements we made before we used a complex, grammatical language? Before linguistic thinking? Since we have had a phenomenal evolution, our ancestors must have made some good judgements.

Conscious vs. Unconscious

Morton Hunt in *The Universe Within* explains conscious and unconscious thought from Donald Norman's point of view as follows:

> Donald Norman, director of the Program in Cognitive Science at the University of California at San Diego, takes a less troubling and more widely accepted stand. He believes that we are aware of some of what lies behind our conscious thoughts but that it is greatly to our advantage to have the unconscious take charge much of the time. "Conscious thought processes," he says, "are very powerful but very slow." Skilled performance, which we need constantly, is fast, but it depends on not doing conscious thinking. The airline pilot, the musician, the juggler, and the typist all rely on automatic skills, because if they had to consciously think about what they're doing, they couldn't do it.[3]

How can we further develop our abilities to make judgements and have a more successful life? How can we use our arms and legs; our hands and fingers; how can we use our bodies to enhance communication and integration between the two hemispheres of our brain; besides meditation, yoga, and Sufi dancing. I recommend studying and using this book and others like it; some of the solutions can be simple. What does sitting up straight do for our nervous system? What goes on when we take a walk and "think things over?" Experiment. Finding out how you operate in life should be one of your most important objectives.

The Awareness Point of View

Left Brain Awareness

The little voice we have inside, often called "internal dialogue," is always chatting away (whether we listen for it or not). Its the chatter we turn off when we meditate. We can think thoughts using words, put them into a grammatical construction, change our minds and change our thoughts, ask questions, arrive at conclusions, and at times, even confuse ourselves. We haven't thought the same since we developed language.

Right Brain Awareness

The right brain is more ancient than the left, in fact both hemispheres used to be right brains with little difference between them. When lateralization began, the left brain gave us handedness. It's interesting the way that this happened. The left brain connects to the right hand. As we became bipedal, we began to gesture more with our hands, the right hand predominantly, causing language to develop in the left hemisphere. We don't know why we favored the right hand but there is good evidence that right handedness caused language to develop in the left hemisphere.

The right brain evolved too, but differently. The right brain became better at judging distance, depth perception, movement, throwing spears, geometry, map making, and designing concepts of time. Not to mention controlling emotions, interacting socially, and singing around camp fires; later in giant cathedrals. The language that the right brain is capable of is a few simple words of an emotional nature. The right brain is more of a feeler, observer, experiencer, than a thinker (in linguistic terms).

Have you ever walked into another room to do something and forgot what you came to do— your right brain got you there but your left brain forgot why— there was a momentary disconnect between the two.

Body awareness comes predominantly from the right brain. It is aware of both sides of the body while the left hemisphere is only aware of the right side. Physical movement is a great way of getting both the left brain and the right brain involved in mental activities. Later you will use spatial associations (where you actually walk to different positions on the floor) to integrate the two hemispheres and make the Self-Evolutionary process a complete experience.

Cat Awareness

My two cats are aware. They know how I treat them and usually communicate approval with their purring. I doubt that they have a *conscious* strategy for success but they might have. They know how to get me to feed them but they haven't figured out what they like to eat yet.

Refer to the *Appendix* on page 165 for detailed explanations of brain function.

What Awareness Brings

We can create subjective experience; ideas with images, sounds, feelings, tastes, smells, and language. We can recall a scene from the past where we expressed a strong belief and use it as a "reference experience" for a belief that needs more authority. We can recall a feeling of "excellence" from the past and use it in the present to perform a task, and be at our best while doing it. This is the stuff of success. Its easy for most people to create an image of their favorite chair, how it feels to sit in it, and what it sounds like when the fire in the fireplace crackles and burns; the smell and taste of eggnog. But how do we create movies in our minds? Are a series of scenes speeded up the way that we project frames in a movie projector? My guess is that both hemispheres are heavily involved and I don't need to know exactly how it's done. I just need to become a better director, actor, and producer of my subjective experience.

Power of the Unconscious

The validity of a two brain approach to life has been acknowledged since the 60s when the puzzling effects of split-brain surgery were being investigated by Dr. R. W. Sperry and his colleagues. They found that cutting the corpus callosum, splitting the two hemispheres of the brain in two (to control the spread of epileptic seizure activity) caused surprising results. Some patients began to act as if they had two separate minds, two separate spheres of consciousness. Further research indicated that the two hemispheres functioned differently and were not just redundant entities that functioned the same. Tons of research followed and some very interesting questions were asked. Is lateralization (the difference in functional between the two hemispheres) an advantage or disadvantage for human endeavors? Terrence Deacon makes an important point in his book: *The Symbolic Species*.

The structure of languages has probably evolved to take advantage of intrinsic subtle biases in developing brains to break up and distribute their component cognitive computations so that they can most easily be processed in parallel, and one important way this can be accomplished is by "*assigning*" functions to either side of the cerebral hemispheres.[4]

Parallel Processing

Parallel processing is intriguing especially considering the number of components that run in parallel in the human brain. The corpus callosum is a bundle of about 50 to 100 million nerve fibers (depending on who counts them) about four inches long and shaped like a pencil. This vast number of connections link to the vast number of neurons that make up the different components of the two hemispheres. More neurons than particles in the universe, some believe. The number of connections and the number of components staggers the imagination but leads me to believe that the super computer in our skulls (which has parallel processing) is leaps and levels above the super computers we build (which also have parallel processing). Enough brain power for us to create and show movies in our minds of events we want to come true and create the circumstances that will cause them to happen.

How much awareness did our ancestors have? They were probably as curious then as we are now. They had a very strong will to survive, did best when challenged, but what did they think of themselves? If anything. They must have been aware of their five senses but did they count them (it would only have taken one hand). I wonder if they wondered what there might be besides the five senses? We know that they began burying their dead about 100,000 years ago but what does it take to think spiritually? An awareness of death is a good clue but how do we get beyond time and space? Do we have to give up our temporal-sequential thinking? Do we have to go beyond dividing time and space and transcend it? Oh my God.

The Process Further Defined

- We know that we have conscious and unconscious awareness and that most of our thinking is done at the level of unconscious awareness, automatically. Since we do most of our thinking unconsciously, and since we have such a narrow window for conscious thought, it is of great advantage for us to program many of our unconscious thoughts.

- We also know that we have two hemispheres in our brain that operate differently in many respects. Both hemispheres help us divide time and space as we go about our business but that the left hemisphere is more "time" oriented and the right hemisphere is more "space" oriented which makes for a very good arrangement.

- We learned from Terrance Deacon that lateralization of the two hemispheres, rather than being a detriment to brain function, breaks up our thought processes so that "they can most easily be processed in parallel..." Lateralization, then, is power processing.

Endnotes

1. P. Russell, *The Brain Book* (New York: Penguin Books USA, 1979).

2. J. Jaynes, *The Origin of Consciousness in the Break-Down of the Bicameral Mind* (Boston: Houghton Mifflin Company, 1977). p37

3. M. Hunt *The Universe Within* (New York: Simon and Schuster, 1982).

4. T. Deacon, *The Symbolic Species* (New York: W. W. Norton & Company, Inc.,1997).

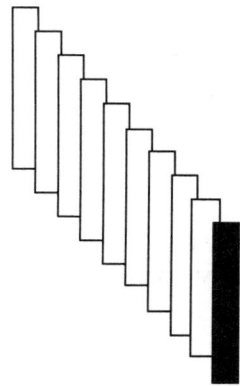

Mental Tools

Nikola Tesla, a Croatian-born American electrical engineer who made alternating current practical (the electricity we use in our houses), was a genius. He had the ability to design electrical-mechanical systems, generators and motors that ran on alternating current rather than direct current (Thomas Edison's choice). He used complicated electrical and mechanical formulas which he often had to formulate himself. He could see the systems operating, how much power they consumed, and calculate how much force they provided. He could see how much his creations would wear in a given period of time and how to extend their life by taking preventive measures. He could see the precise dimensions of his mechanisms and how minute changes would make them better; all in his mind.

He believed that alternating current, as opposed to direct current, was the best way to generate and use electricity. And after Edison rejected him and his ideas, he decided to go it alone and did so. He didn't do as much experimentation as Edison. He had a genius for selecting the best strategy and he could project mental models of complete electrical arrays into the future with precision. His ideas in this area were superior to Edison's and he has since been vindicated, in some cases it took a while. The Erie Lackawanna Railroad in New Jersey was finally converted from direct current to alternating current in the early 1980s. Your toaster, television, and refrigerator run on alternating current. Tesla had his own template.

Use Tesla, Einstein, a favorite teacher, or anyone else who can "be of value" as a model because modeling works. But in the final analysis, it is what you can get to happen "in your life" that counts. There may be thousands of ideas and techniques that will help you develop your ability to succeed but you have to believe in them, value them, own them; they have to become part of your intestines for big challenges in you life to be met.

> The brain loves to take direction. The more precisely, logically, lucidly, cogently, thoroughly, and enthusiastically you direct it, the more successful the results.

Monitoring Thoughts

One of the major differences between living a life of check stubs and rent receipts, waiting for a retirement village or a grassy view and *pursuing* a meaningful life, is in the thinking process. So what is a thought?

> The American Heritage Dictionary defines thought as: "a product of thinking; idea; notion."

Does each thought have a visual as well as an linguistic component? When I think of breakfast and visualize two eggs, is this the usual turn of events? What comes to your mind when you think of breakfast? And how about the feelings; we're always feeling something, aren't we? When I think about the young spinach shoots that the rabbits ate, see the remaining stubs sticking up, I feel anger in my guts. Until I think about the new 18-hole golf course; a mile from the house. If you feel sad, what happens if you sit or stand straight and then look slightly upward and think of something that you are proud of?

Multiple Thoughts

The next question might be: "can we think two thoughts at once?" We can do several things at once; walk, talk, and juggle. It's an intriguing question, some thoughts are so subtle, just a glimmer—too faint to remain in memory longer than a second.

I use the analogy of an airport with only one runway in my resolution of this issue. Airplanes land and take off, one at a time. Sometimes when the airways get crowded, some of the airplanes might have to go into a holding pattern (hold that thought) and things can get pretty hectic. Sometimes takeoffs have to be aborted (when we've been interrupted). The way I see it, an airplane can be a word or phrase or a complete sentence. Or it can be an image, or feeling; but most often, they are some combination of sensory modalities. I am fascinated by the airplanes that fly so high that I can hardly see them, they're just a glimmer— that I can't get a handle on— Not yet.

One Thing at a Time

There are times when I have to switch my attention from one matter to another, often rapidly; from a phone call with another one trying to get in (call waiting), to speaking to someone, to inserting a command into the computer, and the answer for me is to do one thing at a time. I don't know if we can have two thoughts at once and I have never reached the point in meditation where I have no thoughts at all. Not yet. Sometimes I see just a color or an awareness of a feeling, I don't really feel it but I know it's there. It's very light, cerebral, like a wisp of knowingness.

A definition for a thought process that I like is: "sensory modalities in a temporal-sequential order." I've used the term subjective experience a lot; sequences of images, feelings, sounds, smells, tastes, and words. Thoughts are combinations of the five senses and language; with more layers and possibilities that I can imagine.

Some Definitions

For our purposes, let's divide thoughts into the following:

1. **Questions** - The American Heritage Dictionary defines a question as: "an expression of inquiry that invites or calls for a reply..." Questions are an important part of a success strategy; they can be a catalyst for change. Strong beliefs and strong disbeliefs are usually **not** questioned, especially when a decision has been made and a "course of action" is in progress. Nobody questioned what those radar targets were on that fateful Sunday morning at Pearl Harbor or if the Titanic was really unsinkable. Can I self-publish and have a traditional publisher as well?

2. **Beliefs** - The American Heritage Dictionary defines belief as: "mental act, condition, or habit of placing trust or confidence in

a person or thing; faith." We have religious beliefs based on faith, we have political beliefs based mostly on personality; often one person's superstition is another person's religion. It's the strong beliefs that make us successful but only if they are pointed in the right direction. In the Self-Evolutionary model, the "desire for success" and "deserving to be successful" are very important beliefs. Also in the Self-Evolutionary model, beliefs are **not** reality but visions to reach goals. "If anybody can both self-publish and have a traditional publisher, I can." "You gotta believe."

3. **Decisions** - The American Heritage Dictionary defines decision as: "the passing of judgement on an issue under consideration." A decision is the commitment we make to a belief. In this model for success, decisions are strong commitments, made after alternative options have been considered and disqualified. "You gotta commit."

4. **Projections** - are thoughts, ideas, and visions that we project into the future. What I would look like driving a new car, for instance. Projections are interesting to me because we couldn't project anything if we didn't have a past to draw from. Our memories are a large ingredient for the subjective experiences that we create. Our ancestors waited for the sunrise knowing that it would bring warmth and safety; they remembered what it was like the day before. That was an important step. In the **present** we use knowledge from the **past** to plan and create the **future**. It's a very human thing to be doing. "You gotta project your goals into the future in a compelling manner."

5. **Intuition** - is very efficient in that it doesn't take a lot of work. It just seems to happen. Getting it to happen when you want takes skill. Some neuroscientists think that intuition is the difference in the way that the two hemispheres of our brain think. This difference in thinking sometimes leaves gaps and questions; intuitions are how we fill in the gaps. They are generally thought to be a right brain phenomenon and while some people feel that analysis with the left brain gives intuition balance, others believe and trust them without reservation. The people who say "just do it" are probably relying on their intuition, they're relying on something. "You gotta trust your intuitions for them to work." I like to have a good backup position as well.

Ideas in Space

When I think about the beautiful Big Boy tomatoes that I grew last summer, I see them (I can almost feel them they were so big) in color, on or close to the horizon, about four feet in front of me and slightly to the left; maybe about two feet. I want to hold and squeeze one right now. The smooth texture, the flavor, and the juice that squirted out as I ate them are automatic when I think about them. The whole garden takes up most of my left field of visualization, from the horizon down. That's where I put my garden in my mind.

We have to organize our thinking in order to keep track of what is true, what is false. What happened in the past and what we are going to do in the future have to be separated, it makes it easier to keep appointments, plan projects, and get on with our lives. Much of this organization is reflected out into the space around us.

We began to deal with life by looking out at the world and reacting appropriately. We are highly functional because we can remember events, learn from them, and plan our futures. It is only natural to reflect these memories out into the space around us. That's where events initially happen.

When you think of a green glass full of water, how do you visualize it? It may be just a glimmer, just an outline. Do you visualize it to the left or right, up or down from the horizon. How we visualize, feel, and hear is important when we create subjective experience.

Creating Subjective Experience

Our subjective experience, our thoughts, images, feelings, and internal dialogue represent both the state that we are in at the time, our physical state (including biochemical fluctuations) but also how we are viewing and interpreting the world. (You make shitty decisions when you feel shitty.) Because of the vast amount of information we come in contact with, we have to delete a lot of it to keep from being overwhelmed. A lot of it is generalized so that we can organize it and create some efficiencies in our thinking, like having a concept of a car and a name for it so that we don't have to explain what one is each time we talk about one. Some of it is distorted so that we can use it to keep our view of the world congruent, so we can remain consistent; even when wrong. We like to have things that make sense to us and the left hemisphere will very often interpret and fill in information for the right hemisphere and vice versa. This allows us to have optical illusions and enables magicians to put giant aircraft carriers on stage and then to remove them, right before our very eyes.

Our beliefs, values, and attitudes (who we are) all cause us to "filter out" and "plug in" information to give us our view of reality. The influence of heredity, genetics, parental and cultural persuasions are the tectonic plates of our model of the world. Our memories, the way that we divide time and space, language, and previous decisions all form the continents and countries, the hamlets and villages. And the best news is that subjective experience can be changed and projected into the future; and our lives changed because of it. To quote Dr. R. Joseph again:

> We are still capable of making choices...what we think can actually change our neurochemical environment as well as the actual structure of our brain. If we think new thoughts or think old thoughts in a different way and apply different meanings and interpretations to them, we can expand and stretch the limits that our biological makeup has imposed. This process is called learning. Even a person who is mentally retarded is capable of making choices and being happy.[1]

We need mental tools to make changes and a process to tie them together, like a template, and then some way of embedding our desires deeply into our conscious and unconscious mind. I use spatial associations in the Self-Evolutionary process. The process in this book is designed to create a complete successful experience.

A series of successful experiences can be used to give you a more successful personality, to change your identity, to change your life. The mental tools are explained, below.

Dividing Time and Space

If we look at a large component of life as being the way that we divide time and space, then the left brain is more aware of *time* while the right hemisphere is better at delineating *space*. The left brain processes sequential language much more quickly than the right; information with increments as short as 50 milliseconds between sounds can easily be comprehended. The right brain needs 8 or 10 times longer to process information and the time between sounds needs to be at least 350 milliseconds to maintain the integrity of speech. For this reason, the left hemisphere, which processes both consonants and vowels, needs help from the right hemisphere in perceiving and creating long vowels. The left hemisphere provides the quick dialogue and the right hemisphere provides the slower scene changes, we need both.

Subjective Experience

For the purposes of this book, subjective experience is sensory data that either comes from the outside or is generated with our memories and imagination on the inside, and then, in either case, interpreted in our brains; *subjectively*. You will be generating sensory experience (internally), combining it in a Self-Evolutionary template, projecting it into the future, and then acting it out to achieve your goal.

Sensory Modalities

We build our view of the world using the five senses which are often defined as sensory modalities. Visual, auditory, and feeling are the sensory modalities most often used unless of course you make wine or cook for a living; then the sense of taste and smell become very important.

> The electro-chemical process in our nervous system is the closest that we get to reality.

The information we access from memory has **not** been recorded as we originally received it. We have filters; we delete, distort, and generalize the incoming information according to neurological constraints (how our nervous system developed), social constraints (our culture), and individual constraints (our own personal history). This variability colors our view of the world.

Our minds have the ability to flip from one sensory modality to another. We can see an image of a car, hear the sound of a crash, feel afraid, and say a prayer in a very short period of time, sequentially. We **not** only have temporal-sequential processes as we say one word after another but we also have them in our sensory modalities.

We are also able to combine sensory modalities because of the angular gyrus and connected neuronal pathways in the two hemispheres. This gives us the ability to associate, link, and combine images, feelings, and sounds. Refer to the *Appendix* on page 165 for detailed information about brain function. You can say a prayer with feeling, watch a sunset as you sail across the lake with a warm breeze in the face, and feel uplifted. We have the ability to create multidimensional subjective experience, to think creatively; the stuff of mental movie making.

The utter bliss that I feel breathing while in meditation is spiritual in the traditional sense but it is also a lot of chemicals called endorphins being generated in my brain. They are generated by the techniques that I have learned to use over the years. I have relatives who think meditation is weird and maybe even a little perverse. One person's constraint is another person's magic carpet ride. It's up to us to decide what chemical cocktails we want floating around in our heads and we don't have to ingest anything to get them.

You can also listen for sensory words; visual, auditory, and feeling words as we speak. A person might look down and say "It was the **hardest** day of my life." Sensory words become clues to how a person is thinking. How many people have you seen look down when they are sad and say that they have had "a down day?"

Some Visual Words			
appear	clarity	demonstrate	examine
focus	glance	idea	illusion
image	look	notice	observe
outlook	picture	see	show

Example: "I'm going to **focus** on this issue like a laser beam until it is resolved."

Some Auditory Words			
announce	communicate	discuss	divulge
gossip	inquire	listen	loud
noise	pronounce	remark	rumor
say	sound	speak	tell

Example: "The meeting's at two, it'll be short, I don't have much to **say**."

Some Feeling Words			
feel	grip	hold	motion
pressure	shift	solid	sore
stress	support	tension	tied
touch	unbearable	unsettled	whipped

Example: "I'm beginning to **feel** the **pressure** but if I can just get a **hold** of that lost data, I'll be okay."

Some Olfactory Words			
aroma	bouquet	dank	dusty
essence	fragrance	musty	odor
floral	pungent	reeks	rotten
smells	stench	stinks	sweet

Example: "The **sweet smell** of success."

Some Gustatory Words			
bitter	bland	burnt	delicious
flat	salty	sharp	sour
spicy	sweet	tangy	tasty

Example: "It will be a **bitter** pill to swallow."

Some Unspecified Words			
activate	advise	anticipate	consider
create	decide	develop	indicate
know	manage	motivate	organize
plan	prepare	think	understand

Example: "I am beginning to **understand** sensory words."

Sensory words can be used in conversation to enhance rapport with another person. It's a good way to help become more successful. If you notice someone is using a particular sensory modality a lot (visual, auditory, or feeling), you can match the type of words they are using to make them feel more comfortable. You will be speaking their language, so to speak. If someone says that they would like to "see" your garden. Tell them you will be happy to "show" it to them. If someone asks if you would like to "hear" what happened to them. Tell them to "tell" you about it. If someone says that they are "feeling" lousy. Ask them what's causing their "discomfort."

If someone asks you to "tell" them how to get somewhere, you can ask them if they would like a map but they probably want verbal instructions. If someone asks you to "show" them how to do something, you would naturally demonstrate it rather than describe it. I prefer less conversation when I am having good food or tasting good wine. And don't touch me when I am at the Metropolitan Museum admiring great art. I want to have my visual channel open and unfettered.

Using sensory words is something you can do to strengthen your existing rapport skills, **not** something you should do instead of the rapport skills you have previously developed and have been using successfully. If you have a relationship where you give someone information; a boss or a coworker for instance, it's a good idea to find out how they like to get information. You might be able to tell by their sensory words. You can also ask them.

Your Favorite Sensory System

We usually have one sensory system that we prefer but use all of them. For instance, when I'm learning a procedure of some kind, I like to establish the procedure visually, in steps. Then I like to add language but I like to get the language just right. Then I like to step it off to get the feel of it.

Once I can visualize the process, in the proper sequence, say the language, and have a good feel for it, I can rearrange it. I can compare it with other processes; I own it. I have had people tell me **not** to think about a procedure but to "just do it." I've tried, it doesn't work for me.

I address the golf ball by placing my left foot into position first, then my right. I grip the golf club twice to become comfortable and then relax my back and make sure my feet are firmly in place, **not** on my toes, **not** too far back. I make a conscious effort to look straight down at the ball, perform the swing in my mind, then I move the golf club back and forth twice, set it back down and check my aim. I then monitor my breathing, I want to swing on an exhale. "David, you know how, put the ball straight into the target, make it feel nice, sail that beautiful white ball like a shooting star." I then, at a "top of breath," move my left knee to initiate the swing.

It took me two years to realize that the walks that I like to take, to sort things out, have a very strong "feeling" quality. And of course, as I walk, I work out visual scenarios in my mind complete with dialogue, little movies that I make and edit, rerun, and sometimes discard but they are all done within the feeling concept of walking. (We've been doing this for several million years.) How do you sort out your thoughts?

It's also a very good idea to strengthen the sensory systems that we don't use as much. If you would like to strengthen the visual system, watch the television with the sound off (see how much you can understand; it also eliminates the noise from the commercials). Or close your eyes and just listen to enhance the auditory. Then close your eyes and put ear plugs in your ears to just feel for a while. Pretend that you are blind and deaf, then find your way around your house. Become very curious. Do you talk to yourself as you feel your way around?

What happens when you limit your sensory input? Does your mind begin generating images, sounds, and feelings from the inside? That's what I do and it can be very useful when I want to go inside and explore who I am, what I'm thinking, and to learn new things about myself. Somehow I get a sense of the real me. This a great time to give yourself verbal instructions. It is as if you are all ears.

Get in Touch

 I shut off the radio in my car if I am in an unknown neighborhood searching for an address because it helps me see better; or at least I feel that it does. I'm sure that I concentrate better when I do it. I see better if I relax the backs of my eyeballs and then my whole face, but somehow, and I don't know exactly how, I focus my eyes more strongly in a relaxed manner. It's easier to do this than to describe it. The point I am making is that it's good to become more aware of your subjective experiences (visual, auditory, feeling, smell, and taste), how you think, what makes you the most comfortable when listening, talking, observing, and obtaining goals.

Sensory Sequencing

Sensory sequencing is the way we program our neurology, our brain; the way that we think. I like to think in terms of the five senses plus language. I see a friend, get a good feeling, and remind myself to ask her to dinner. Human behavior then, is the way that we sequence sensory data (internally and externally). We have sensory sequences, thinking processes for milking cows, getting up in the morning, falling in love, buying a house, spelling, and all of the other things we do with our lives. *SET for Success*, at one level, is a way to program sensory sequences (thoughts) to obtain a goal.

Enhancing Subjective Experience

Since we organize information externally, in the space around us, and internally (to fit our model of the world), and since we think in a temporal-sequential manner, we have certain patterns in our thinking. And since we think using sensory modalities; see, hear, feel (taste and smell), we need to use vision, audition, feeling, taste, and smell to enhance and associate our subjective experience, before projecting it into the future. Let's talk about enhancing subjective experience now and associating it later.

Sensory Adjustments

Our five senses can be adjusted. Brightness, size, focus, and clarity of our visual sense can be adjusted. If you are creating a subjective experience to obtain a goal; if you have created an image and auditory effects, along with the appropriate feelings, you can manipulate the senses to enhance the experience. If you want to substitute chewing gum for smoking cigarettes, you can visualize the chewing gum as brighter and clearer. Magnify the good aspects of the gum. "Wouldn't you rather have a clean, good smelling, fresh tasting piece of chewing gum?" You can make the auditory louder or softer, and the feelings can be made more powerful or more subtle; depending on what works best for you. You can tell yourself in a special voice: "How good will you feel having a piece of gum rather than a cigarette?" Double the feeling, double the pleasure. You can then do the opposite for cigarettes. Make them dimmer, smaller, unhealthy, with uncomfortable feelings.

Think of someone you are fond of, realize how you feel about that person. Now make the feeling more powerful, what ever it takes to make you more fond. Have the person speak in an exciting voice; make the image more provocative; these are your feelings, images, and sounds; you are the writer, director, and producer. You can use your senses to adjust your experience. The advertising industry is using them to sell you— you can surely use them to obtain your goals. You really deserve a break today, tomorrow, and for the rest of your life.

Some types of sensory adjustments are listed below.

Visual	Auditory	Feeling
Size	Volume	Pressure
Motion/Still	Tone	Tactile sensations
Location	Tempo	Movement
Bright/Dim	Pitch	Weight
Shape	Location	Location in body
Focused/Unfocused	Harmony	Breathing rate

Enhance Your Feelings

Good feelings from the past are a recipe for ecstasy. They can be regenerated, amplified, and used as part of the overall process described in this book (or used anytime you want to feel good).

We all have galleries of good feelings. We have a treasure trove of experiences to draw on. That first kiss, for instance. There are many "first things" that were wonderful and will be wonderful for the rest of our lives; *in our memories*. But why settle for that? Bring some of them back and have a good time all over again. It's simply a matter of managing resources. Here's how.

Step 1. Remember the feeling.

I remember the feeling I got when I used to smoked pot. It used to begin in the middle of my forehead and spread out, come down my nose and relax my whole jaw. Then it would kind of loop up around my eyes, sink into my head before going down to my feet. Some will read this and wonder if I am promoting pot. **No.** Some might say that I will be enticing people to try or continue using pot. **No.** If drugs have been a part of your life and your can get good feelings from the chemicals in you brain without ingesting anything, it may be a good idea for you. You have probably payed a high price for those feelings, you might want to use them now, safely.

Some people believe any thing that makes us feel good will put us off the deep end. Some of our religions promote feeling bad to obtain that eternal reward. Whether the "pious" do it with good intentions or as a means to gain power over us, too many of us came to believe that bad feelings should be brought up over and over again so that we could stay miserable for days, weeks, months, and years on end. At some point in life, we have to leave the bad feelings behind and learn to accommodate good ones.

Find out how much ecstasy you can stand. You have all the drugs you will ever need to feel good, right inside of your brain. It's called thinking. See how high you can be with just your thoughts and then see how long you can maintain it. Then, associate it to a part of your body (when the feeling is at the maximum, hold your right ear lobe) so that you will be able to access the feeling later when you touch your right ear lobe again. Associating is explained in detail below. I like to associate good things to the bottoms of my feet and then go for a walk. I am especially fond of the feeling I get while breathing in meditation. I associate the feeling to the bottoms of my feet, (it's easy, as I breathe and get that good feeling I become very aware of the bottoms of my feet), then I go for a walk and monitor my feelings. When I am sure that the association is working, the feeling is evident, I then associate it to my whole body and enjoy the walk. How many different ways can you make yourself feel good without ingesting anything? Can you make yourself feel good all day, every day?

Step 2. Regenerate the feeling.

Feelings have a tendency to dissipate. To leak out or flow away. The idea is to trace the feeling through the body and if it wants to go outside the body, or go to a dead end, loop it back around so that it regenerates. After you are accomplished at regenerating your feelings, go to Step 3.

Step 3. Increase the feeling.

This is easy to do but take some time and explore different avenues. I like to tie an increase in feeling to my breath. We do a lot of things with our breathing; like staying alive. I increase the feeling as I inhale and then maintain it when I exhale.

Step 4. Adjust the breath so that you continue to maintain the feeling.

Step 5. Experiment with changing the quality of the feeling.

Can you combine relaxation and expectation together so that

you have great expectations but remain relaxed? We often do our best work when we are cool, collected, confident, and relaxed; except for the times when we need to be excited and full of energy.

Enhancing feelings can be a big help in projecting your success scenarios into the future. Also, when you perform the action that takes you to your goal.

Reminder: Be sure and associate the good feelings you have generated and enhanced to some place on your body so that you will be able to access the feeling later.

Generate Strong Images

In this lifetime and in the evolutionary past, we learned to see before we learned to speak. Some of us have **not** been using our abilities to visualize much and have come to the conclusion that we can't (visualize). In reality, it's like a muscle that needs toning. The visual images are there but the level of awareness needs to be increased.

If you find it difficult to create a picture in your mind, you can imagine a switch much like on your television set. Turn the switch on and slowly turn it up until you see an image or just an outline of an image. If the picture is **not** bright enough, imagine a brightness knob and turn it up until the picture is brighter. Have another knob for making the picture bigger if you need to. Experiment to see what will make it work better. Can you see it in color? Turn the color knob. It works best for me if I make the adjustments slowly. If this is **not** working very well for you; stop, relax and get into that special place you go when you daydream. Let yourself get into that special awareness, daydream about your goal; adjust images, feelings, and sound as appropriate. Let this be easy for you to do. I have never had a hard time making a daydream. Have you?

Maybe this is like a painting that needs to be sketched in from time to time; or like getting into condition, you may need to exercise a little each day. You might want to look at a picture of something, close your eyes, and then recall the picture. Give yourself some time and space if you need to and remember that even very subtle images can be very powerful.

Generate Good Internal Dialogue

We have all been told to think positively, use affirmations, be optimistic, and other good advice. Why **not** make internal dialogue an event. At least some of the time. I've seen estimates that we have 60,000 thoughts a day and I doubt that we can make them all into positive, colorful, profound experiences that will propel us to new heights in happiness and prosperity. We can certainly have better internal dialogue which can help lead to new heights in happiness and prosperity.

Some of us talk to ourselves as if we were strangers or peasants or naughty school children. Let's begin with the premise that we are "our own best friends" and having a good relationship with ourselves is a priceless resource. Then let's presuppose that the brain, indeed the whole nervous system loves to take direction. Let's then assume that if a positive thought is of value that a series of positive thoughts, that lead to a particular goal, are even more valuable.

> I'm a good student. I need a better average. I need to become a better student. I'm going to learn how to learn better. I deserve to learn better. I deserve to be the best that I can be. We are all genetically programed for success, I just need to work this out. I know that I can do it. This is it. I'm going to take the study course for learning that was announced. I'm going to sign up for it right after class. This is real, I'm real, I'm going to make this happen. I'm going to be an excellent student. I can't wait to get started. I'm going to be on the Dean's List. I see myself getting good grades, all A's this semester.

There is a lot more here than positive thinking, isn't there? This is an example of temporal-sequential processing, one thought after another, in this case they become more positive and lead to a goal. The brain loves this kind of direction. Refer to the following graphic:

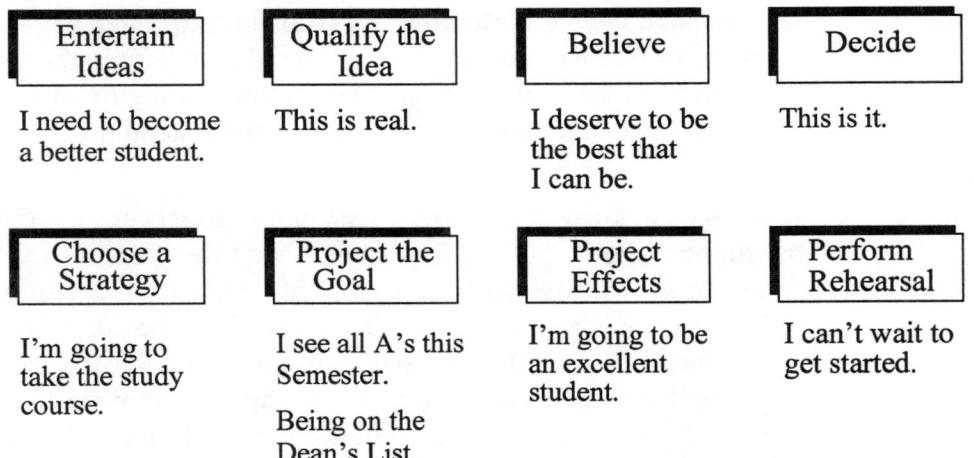

Entertain Ideas	Qualify the Idea	Believe	Decide
I need to become a better student.	This is real.	I deserve to be the best that I can be.	This is it.

Choose a Strategy	Project the Goal	Project Effects	Perform Rehearsal
I'm going to take the study course.	I see all A's this Semester. Being on the Dean's List.	I'm going to be an excellent student.	I can't wait to get started.

Now, can you imagine someone saying the above sequence of thoughts in a monotone, without feeling? Wouldn't it be better to add more tone, tempo, and emotion into our internal dialogue so that it resonates better? Many less successful people think in negative terms, in harsh tones, and even though some of us do it at times, it's much better to think in positive terms; and instead of one positive thought, might as well string them together and have them lead to a goal.

Experiment with your internal dialogue. When is it best to have a soft loving tone, a firm tone, a conciliatory tone, or an exciting tone? There's more than internal dialogue here isn't there? This is about the relationship we have with ourselves. And you could add more to this event (that began as a positive thought), you could associate it to some part of your body so that it really becomes part of you. Associating is our next topic.

Associate Subjective Experience

We use two types of associations in this book: simple associations and spatial associations. An association, in either case, is one experience being associated, linked, or anchored with another. For Pavlov ringing a bell and feeding the dogs. After a while, the dogs would salivate when the bell was rung without any food being given. When I think of a time in the past when I was in a state of excellence and hold my right ear lobe, I am using a simple association. For spatial associations, a space becomes one of the experiences. Like the experience of getting married being associated with the place where the marriage took place, in a church in many cases. We use spaces on the floor marked with the components of the Self-Evolutionary template as spatial associations. Refer to *How Associations Work* on page 173 for a detailed description of what happens in the brain when associations are made.

Simple Associations

You will probably be using touch and associate it with a subjective experience. You can think of a strong belief and use it as a reference to enhance another belief; you would be using a strong belief to enhance a weaker belief. For example:

Step 1. Think of a strong, reference belief "I deserve to be the best that I can be," for instance.

Step 2. What does it look like (I see a white space moving upward)?

Step 3. What does it sound like (I say it in a low measured voice)?

Step 4. What does it feel like (I feel excitement).

Step 5. What does it smell or taste like (nothing for me)?

Step 6. Touch and hold your right ear lobe (or another part of your body) when you feel, see, and hear it the most intense. You have just associated that belief to your right ear lobe.

Step 7. While you are still holding your right ear lobe, think about the new belief, the belief you want to enhance. You have associated the new belief to the right ear lobe.

Step 8. After you are comfortable thinking about the new belief, make the sensory modalities (visual, auditory, feeling etc.) the same as the other (reference) belief, if they are not already the same. And you can adjust them to make both beliefs even stronger.

Step 9. You can make the images clearer, brighter, more colorful; sound can be more pleasant or more uplifting; feelings more positive.

The following points are important when installing and firing off associations.

1. Timing is critical. Install the association when the subjective experience (feelings, images, sounds etc.) are the most intense.

Remember to really let yourself have a full experience.

2. In the context of this book and programming yourself for success, you will be associating your subjective experiences to each component of a Self-Evolutionary template and then you will tie all of the components of your template together using spatial associations.

3. Soft music and dim lights can be external associations. Someone patting you on the back is an external association. You are creating or firing off an association every time you pet your dog or cat; scold or compliment your child. Internal associations can be anything that you can imagine. If you are trying to develop a cordial relationship with a neighbor, think of a good friend when you look at him. Life is full of associations. Make associations that are to your advantage.

4. Associations can be stacked. If you want to create a state of excellence within, you can recreate the subjective experience of a time when you were in a state of excellence and then associate it. The time you asked your boss for a raise and got it, for instance, can be associated to the act of stroking you chin or feeling the area between two fingers. You can then stack a number of experiences (when you were in a state of excellence) and use the same association point. This makes for a very strong, stacked association. You might want to fire off the association when you go into a meeting, interview, or a negotiation.

5. Fire off the association the same as you installed it. If you use an ear lobe for instance, hold it with approximately the same pressure.

6. The stronger the initial subjective experience, the stronger the response will be when you fire off the association.

7. You can enhance any subjective experience with sensory adjustments. You can even make a movie out of subjective experience and then enhance the movie. You could make a movie of buying a house in your mind and then go and buy it. Be sure to get into a state of excellence when you negotiate price.

8. You can repeat the association process to reinforce it, especially if the association hasn't been used for a period of time.

Spatial Associations

The instructions for using the spatial associations in the Self-Evolutionary process are given in the *Implement Your Self-*

Evolutionary Template chapter. The Self-Evolutionary template becomes associated in your mind, in the proper sequence, and thus schedules you for success.

Classrooms and schools can be very strong spatial associations as can battlefields, houses, and your favorite restaurant. What happens to you when you visit the old neighborhood, school, or the ship you once served on. These can be very strong associations whether you visit them in person or as you drive to work or walk through the park.

Project Subjective Experience

The reason for creating and enhancing subjective experience in this model is to project it into the future so that the brain can act on it. When you store a goal in the future part of your mind (and become hungry to have it) you are likely to obtain your goal. You can envision the goal being obtained next month, or the next time that your boss treats you badly, or the next time you plant your garden, or in five minutes. Your time concept can give you a precise time period but sometimes it is appropriate to just put goals "out there where they need to be."

Time

When did we first keep track of time? I have visions of our ancestors making notches on a stick to count the days.

The Calendar

How many times the sun comes up and goes down is counted on calendars. (It's **not** the only way to count time, the Native Americans counted moons as well.) After watching the solar system for a while we became more sophisticated and arranged the days into weeks, months, and years. And when we invented a calendar on the outside, we also created one on the inside (of our mind). I think we created the one on the inside first. You can call the calendar on the inside your "time concept." We all have different ways of representing time including lines, arcs, and circles. The greater sophistication came when we reflected the time on the inside back to the outside. This is where it's the most useful to us.

Visualization of Time

How do you visualize the seven days of the week? Just stop

and think about a day of the week and what comes to mind. My week is a circle with seven little windows. Sunday is on top. I see the year as a bigger circle. I view it as if I am in the middle. When I think of the years in this century, I see them as lines that bend every 20 years but they are all represented in front of me. It probably has something to do with the way that time was explained to me when I was young. I am a "view time" person, I see both the past and the future in front of me. Stop and think about where you imagine your future. Is the future in front and the past in back? Is the future bright or dark? Maybe you will want to lighten it up using sensory adjustments.

Those of you who think that you don't think visually, think again. Think about the color of your first car or your baby's face the very first time you saw it. We all think visually even if we prefer to think in terms of sound or feeling. It's always a blend, multimodal, a many splendorous thing.

We have to organize our mental maps, our thoughts and memories, to get along in life. The way that we organize the past and future is reflected outside of us in the space around us. This allows us to get a handle on it. This is a touch of genius on our part.

Subjective experience can usually be visualized with the eyes either open or closed. I don't actually see leaf lettuce out in front of me when I think of my garden last year but I do see an *image* of leaf lettuce. It's a vivid memory with taste and texture associated with it. When I think of the word "book," I see a little image of a book in my left field of visualization. It's small, just an outline, very subtle, enough to denote the concept. When I think of Tuesday I see the letters of the word Tuesday in a little window, the second window from Sunday. It's a symbolic abstraction that helps me to keep track of the days of the week so that I can keep the appointments with the veterinarian for my two cats. Their time concepts are confined to meals and going out at night which works very well for them.

Language

Language reflects the way that we organize experience.

"Lets put this behind us."

"We'll take it one step at a time."

"My mind goes back to Lorient."

"The future keeps getting brighter."

"I was beside myself with joy."

"That was when I reached a turning point."

"I have a new outlook on life."

The point is that if we can organize things in this manner, we can reorganize them, we can restructure ourselves by using these images along with the associated sensory modalities. And we can do it simply and eloquently and feel good every time we breathe.

Establishing Your Time Concept

Projecting your goal into the future schedules you for success. If you are going to project a goal into the future, you have to know where you "view or envision" the future.

View Time and Envision Time

Most people either "view time" or "envision time."

View time is when the entire time concept; past, present, and future is visualized in front (usually with the past to the right and the future to the left). View time people usually keep appointments more easily than envision time people.

Envision time is when people live more in the present; are less aware of time. The body (or part of the body) represents part of their time concept, (usually the present, with the future in front and the past in back). If you have an appointment with an envision time person, call and remind them. They may get involved in what they are doing and forget.

There are variations and it may take some time to discover exactly how you represent time in your mind but time is relative and it will happen relatively quickly even if you can only sketch in part of it, initially. If it changes as you work on it, relax, it will settle down. You have been using time for most of your life but this is the first time you are making a full presentation of your time concept to your conscious mind. Take your time, do whatever works for you.

Draw Your Time Concept

Draw your time concept in your mind and then on paper and if it doesn't come to you easily, I suggest that you first decide where the past feels the most comfortable for you. Take a guess if you aren't sure. Think of something that happened last week, last month, or last year and see where your attention goes. When you have problems, do you think about putting them behind you? When you think of kindergarten, grade school, or high school, where does your attention go? In which direction do you look? If you were to float up and go back to a time in the past, where would you float to? Where do you feel the most comfortable envisioning the present? In your body? In front of you? Where is the future? Sketch in these areas. You can add details later.

For our purposes now, it is only necessary that you know where the future is. I often create a goal in my mind and then declare that I want it to exist for the rest of the day, the rest of the week, the rest of the month, the rest of the year, the rest of my life as I visualize these different time periods. The mind loves to take direction.

Project into the Future

It helps to be in a positive mood when you do any of these techniques and you know how to create positive feelings. Reread this chapter as necessary.

Sometimes I project goals into the future while in my car or while walking across a parking lot going to a meeting. Here is an idea. Project a goal into the future a week before you are going to actualize it. Then do it again the night before. You may even want to project it again when you first get up in the morning, the day that you are going to accomplish it. This scenario gives your unconscious time to work things out and make adjustments as the time gets closer.

Assumptions

The brain loves to take direction; indeed the whole nervous system does. The nervous system includes the 3-pound brain within the skull (the most complex system known to man), the brain in the stomach, and maybe even brains in our other organs. Every fiber in our body contains information and communicates with the rest of the body. The Self-Evolutionary process provides a way to program our five senses (our sensory modalities) and our language to enhance and inhibit behavior.

It is an excellent way to give the nervous system direction but what gives the Self-Evolutionary process its direction?

1. If it is possible for one, it is possible for all. If it is possible for anyone, it is possible for you. We as humans have roughly the same genetic structure and function about the same. Some with very low IQs will be limited in what they can do and many have emotional problems that place limits on them. There is also variability in circumstances: **not** all of us have unlimited funds for instance but by and large, "if anybody can do it, you can do it." And we all deserve to be the best that we can be.

2. Individuals have all the resources they need to achieve their goals. If **not** the exact resources they need, the potential to obtain them by modeling and other generative techniques including creating and enhancing subjective experience. This assumption is similar to many eastern spiritual paths that believe that spiritual growth is a matter of letting what is already instilled within us to unfold. Also, there is nothing inside of us that we can or should want to get rid of. The part of us causing the most negative responses may cause the most positive responses when redirected.

3. All behavior has an original intention. When alcoholics first begin to drink, it does something good for them, makes them feel good. However alcoholism is handled, keeping the original intention and finding a healthy way of fulfilling it is a sound strategy. There are many ways to feel good without drinking alcohol. When a particular behavior begins to produce unwanted results, it's time for a change and the more choices, the more options, the better.

4. People make the best choices available to them. We are genetically programmed to survive and prosper. Yes, we have challenges. We, just like our parents may **not** have had as many choices as they would have liked. And we have cultural biases but we are still capable of making choices and we all want to have successful and happy lives. We may have to rethink a myriad of unfortunate perspectives that we learned when we were too young to know the difference. If you were told that successful people think that "they are better that others," for instance, you may need to rethink that idea in order to feel good about yourself being successful. If someone has told you that you should suffer in this life so that you can go to heaven, you may want counseling. We have to determine what we should be

responsible for and what really works for us before we can make the best choices.

5. We are all connected and we all interact on many levels. We as a people are systemic and mutually influence one another. This is why we have cheer leaders for sports and why gossip can be so destructive.

6. Entities self-organize and seek states of balance and stability. Water seeks its own level, friends hang together, and we can organize our thoughts to obtain goals within the Self-Evolutionary process.

7. There are no failures, only feedback. If we make mistakes and move on we are likely headed toward our goal. If we allow "ourselves" to make mistakes and move on we should allow "others" to do the same. Many politicians don't learn this. They prefer to bicker and dig up dirt on their opponents rather than carrying out the people's business.

The Process Further Defined

1. We know that our thoughts are reflected out into the area around us providing time concepts and other mental organization.

2. We know that a large, important part of our thinking is done in a temporal-sequential manner, one thought after another. We also know that our sensory modalities (images, sounds, feelings, smells, and tastes) plus language are the discrete components that are sequenced.

3. The Language Axis **not** only decodes the language we hear but also creates the language we speak, to ourselves and to others. Refer to the *Appendix* on page 165 for details. This language, along with associated images and feelings, via the angular gyrus, produces multimodal thinking. Multimodal thinking (with the left and right hemispheres) is how we create subjective experience, time concepts, the ability to project into the future, and to use simple and spatial associations. It is also how we bring up images, feelings, and sounds in our minds so that we can manipulate them using sensory adjustments.

4. The left hemisphere gives us dialogue with words following each other quickly while the right hemisphere provides the pictures, the feelings, the melody; how every thing is arranged in

space. This arrangement gives us the ability to bring all of the components of subjective experience together; we are the writer, director, and producer of flawless movies in our minds.

5. Scenes flow in our movies with automatic camera angles (right hemisphere), the dialogue doesn't have to be dubbed in, it's automatic (from the left hemisphere). The feelings come and go as the melody of sensation is created from within. We save the child, make a fortune on wall street, shoot a 70 in golf, win the affection of someone we love; and become successful, if we choose to. To quote Mark McGwire after the last game of the 1998 baseball season when he hit his 69th and 70th, record breaking home runs: "If you put your mind to something, it will happen."

6. You have all of the mental equipment, all of the emotion and passion that you need, you have been genetically programmed for success, you only need to become a stronger writer, director, and producer of your life. As you become more competent at creating your subjective experiences and projecting them into the future, the more you will be able to bring goals from the movies of your mind to the reality of your life. The brain loves to take direction. The better and more complete the direction, the more successful you will be. The next three chapters show you how to give your brain direction.

Endnotes

1. R. Joseph, *The Right Brain and the Unconscious* (New York: Plenum Press, 1992).

SET for Success is unique in that it teaches you to take your subjective experience, your visions, feelings, and language for success and enhance it, superimpose it on the Self-Evolutionary template, project it into the future, and then get into a state of excellence to achieve your goal.

Part Two

This is the how-to section. It begins with an overview and then explains exactly how to design a Self-Evolutionary template, a blueprint for obtaining your goal. You are then taught how to implement your Self-Evolutionary template; (how to embed it deeply in your conscious and unconscious awareness) so you can more easily perform tasks, more easily obtain your goal.

If it is arrogant for me to believe that I can teach you to put the necessary ingredients for success (beliefs, decisions, strategies, etc.) into templates that will make you more successful, I am ready to take that chance.

The brain loves to take direction; it does it exquisitely, faithfully. The brain collects information from you and the outside world as it helps you to mobilize resources to meet challenges. The more detailed, cogent, logical, and enthusiastic the direction is, the more successful you will be.

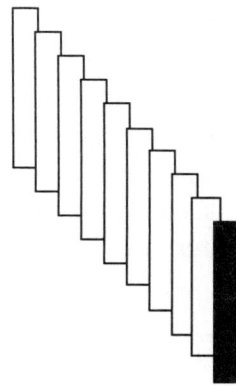

Overview

The intelligence that created the universe gives us the right and the responsibility to be who we are. It also gives us the right to be who we want to become. There will always be someone who wants to discourage us from reaching our goals. This is natural since *we all* have our views of the world pointing in different directions. We all have our own agendas and the instinct for survival is strong and that's good. It's also good when people try to discourage us because it gives us the opportunity to show them the "mettle" that we are made of. "You gotta have pluck."

No spelled backwards is "on." If someone tells you "no," that something can't be done or you can't do it, consider turning the letters around and get "turned on" to do it.

It's easy to be turned on, to be strengthened when we have encouragement from others. Please use all of the encouragement you can get but it is also important to conquer adversity, all alone, when need be. We sometimes need to "bite the bull dog."

You have the power and the stability of the universe supporting you. You have millions of years of genetic evolution in every cell of your body. You are part of the gene pool that has created the Mona Lisa, has mapped the solar system, has flown satellites to each of the planets, and placed a telescope into space that can "almost" see the edge of time. You are part of the evolution that is going to fly to Mars and beyond. You are part of, and have a vested interest in humankind's future accomplishments but you have an even greater vested interest in your own future.

> 1. You will follow the directions in the next chapter to design a Self-Evolutionary template which means putting your subjective experience including visual, auditory, and feeling perceptions onto a series of Design Sheets. Each Design Sheet represents a different component of success.
>
> 2. You will then use the *Implement Your Self-Evolutionary Template* chapter to install the template deeply in your conscious and unconscious awareness. You will use the Design Sheets to do this along with spatial associations.

What is Success?

Success is what you determine it to be. For some people success is finding that they want to become a veterinarian and then become one. To others, success is developing a successful personality so that success becomes second nature. Others want to remove limits that have been frustrating them since childhood. They want to remove the imprint of the 3rd grade teacher, for instance. The one that spoke like Betty Davis and said they weren't smart enough to write well or be good at mathematics.

Some want to accept life on its terms letting it flow through them so that life is the teacher nudging them toward further development. Others want to take a bite out of life and reach for the golden ring. For others, happiness is being content with what they have and maintaining it.

Some yogis seem to stop all signs of life with no discernible pulse and remain buried for days. When it comes time for them to be removed from the earth, their vital signs reappear and they go on with their lives. It makes some of the scientists scratch their heads. I scratched my head when I first read about it. Can this really be true? How much can we affect deep biological responses, recover from debilitating illness, overcome obstacles, and become as successful as we want to. How can we break the habit of procrastinating, being afraid of success, thinking poorly of others; how much can we change our lives?

On one hand we can be very conservative in our thinking, look for scientific proof in all that we experience, and stay within well established behaviors whether they work or not. On the other hand, why not harvest the placebo effect. If people believe that a pill will make them better, it will roughly 35% of the time, even when the pill is made of inert substances, so why not harvest that belief system?

We have been endowed by God, nature, the universe (whatever the reality of creation is for you) with a super computing brain, a tremendous amount of power in our beliefs and decisions, and the ability to develop beautiful, powerful, strategies. We, as a race have been successful for many thousands of years. It seems to me that it is time to take some of the thinking that the human race has been using for success and define a process that we can use, individually.

How do we make changes within? What changes would we like to make? Would we want to change where we were born and raised, the religion we were endowed with (or subjected to), our education and life experiences, if we could? How much can we change who we are?

Can we evolve quickly in one step, to a level above our present experience, or is it best to replace the wall of life one brick at a time? Should we change our identity first and wait for the behavior to follow or change the behavior so that the identity follows? The unconscious has a tendency to look at behavior and come to its own conclusions. Behavior is often a good way to program the unconscious. "Say it until it becomes true," so to speak.

These are issues that you will work through as you use the Self-Evolutionary process. You will decide what is best for you. You will evolve as you want to, as you need to.

Can you be self-evolutionary, after learning to use the process in this book. Can you decide to develop your potential and maybe even exceed it? We don't really know what our potential is until we begin to develop it and who says that we can't develop more potential? Developing more potential for ourselves, is that arrogant or real? I believe that you will evolve in some fashion, with or without this process. I believe that this process gives you much more control; it allows you to become Self-Evolutionary.

> Can you better your relationship with your mind and the minds of others?

The Self-Evolutionary Components

There are nine components, each with different mental functions. There is also a reference component. You will design (create mental functions for) and then implement (embed in memory) all of the components. This gives your brain direction to obtain your goal. The brain loves to take direction. The more precisely, logically, lucidly, cogently, thoroughly, and enthusiastically you direct it, the more successful the results. The order that I have put the components into are what seems like the most natural. If a different order works best for you, please feel free to change the order. You might want to stay with the original order until you gain some experience with the process.

1. **Entertain Ideas**. This component is where you record how you obtained the idea for your goal. The idea might have come from insight or a nagging reminder of a problem; it might have been around for years or it might have come out of the blue and be as fresh as new snow. If someone is diagnosed as diabetic, they can be forced into a "change of life-style" to maintain their health. On the other hand, someone may decide that they are not as fulfilled as they would like to be as a doctor and may go into politics. A combat infantrymen from Desert Storm may decide to become a male nurse as a result of his war experiences. We are all on a journey making choices everyday. How the choices are made is important and can tell us a lot about ourselves. If you keep being forced to act, maybe you're not proactive enough, for instance. How you entertain ideas (decide what is important) reflects your values and beliefs, indeed your identity. When you

become more aware of how you entertain ideas, you understand yourself better. That's important.

2. **Qualify an Idea**. This is where you take the idea that you want to pursue (your goal) and ensure that it is a good thing to do (is not likely to cause problems.) This component is also designed to see if you really want to accomplish the goal. Sometimes we get a benefit from an otherwise undesirable situation and don't really want to change. Someone with Chronic Fatigue Syndrome might want to avoid getting well so they won't have to go back to a job they hate. Desire and commitment might be missing from their recovery process.

3. **Believe**. This is where you believe, really believe that you are going to be successful in the pursuit of your goal. Since the idea has been qualified, it is one you can believe in, strongly. If this process is followed carefully, you will be able to establish a belief in your recovery from alcoholism, a debilitating disease, an eating disorder, or shooting a 70 in golf. If you know in your heart that you can accomplish your goal, you can.

4. **Decide**. This is where you eliminate the possibility that there is a better idea than the one you have chosen to pursue and then make a firm decision. It is a brain storming process and a decision process. This is where you make a powerful decision; this is where you make a firm commitment. Someone with arthritis might look at diet, medication, exercise, a new drug, or a new treatment program, for instance; before making the final decision on the treatment or combination of treatments. All of the options should be looked at before committing resources. This is in one sense like a strategy but I call the means of carrying out the decision a strategy.

5. **Choose a Strategy**. This is where you choose the strategy or strategies that will "take you to your goal." You already have the process in this book as part of the strategy (an element of the overall strategy). This, like Decide, is a brain storming session and a decision process. If a diabetic, with the help of a medical professional decides to use diet to maintain good health, how is the diet implemented? Who is going to cook; what? The person responsible for the meals might use books, medical advice, the internet, and software programs. I have a diabetic friend who loves to watch the "cooking shows" on television.

6. **Project the Goal.** This is where you project your goal into the future, in the appropriate time frame; by image, feeling, and

sound (smell and taste per your appetite). This is where you project your vision into the time that is to come, the future, in a COMPELLING manner. Stroke patients may see, hear, and feel function return to their body. A heart attack patient may see, hear, and feel a normal life with both work and recreation. The president of the company may see a well organized efficient organization. An artist may see a one person show. The more compelling the projection, the better chance for success. A project at work may have a deadline. You can project exactly what will happen when the deadline arrives and the enterprise is completed successfully. You can make a movie in full panoramic, stereophonic sound. If you choose to lose10 pounds in three weeks you can see yourself walking up to the scale and measuring your desired weight.

7. **Project the Effects.** This is where you project the effects of your goal into the future, in the appropriate time frame, by image, feeling, and sound (smell and taste per your appetite). The effects are usually longer term than the goal that produced them. A diabetic may want to not only feel better but regain health and live a full life. Someone investing for retirement may want to see their assets appreciate. A cancer patient may want to live past five years so that the odds for a complete life are enhanced. A smoker may look forward to 15 smoke-free years when the lungs are back to normal.

8. **Performance Rehearsal.** This is where you create and preview a very powerful "mental state" (whether it be excitement, focus, joy, relaxation, or some combination of states) that you will be in when you actually perform the task needed to obtain your goal. Athletes do this perhaps better than anybody but they don't have a monopoly on it. Alcoholics can rehearse the state that they need to be in to say "no" to a drink and stay sober for another day. A salesman can design a mental state for closing a sale. A person recovering from a stroke can find a "determination state" to get into for therapeutic sessions. Diabetics might need a special "motivational state" to stick to their diet.

9. **Analyze the Results.** Analyze the results of the performance to see how it can be made better. Maybe you needed a stronger belief or a better strategy; did you really want the goal bad enough? This is where you enhance the process and when it's time, perform it again. Maybe with more determination or projecting it into the future in a more compelling manner.

If you are satisfied with the results, move on to the next adventure. If it is something that you do once, like make a speech accepting an honor, or interviewing for a great job, or celebrating a 50th Wedding Anniversary, rehearse it several times. Your brain can give you excellent feedback for events that you create in your mind, if you ask for it. If going for a job interview you may want to rehearse it under different contexts so that you will be ready for different circumstances. You might rehearse several ways of asking for the job or try answering different questions about your qualifications. If you are going to propose marriage, you might want to get some advice from a woman; if you are a man proposing to a woman.

The Self-Evolutionary Process

It is a flexible, generic process and will need to be used differently at different times throughout a large project. The focus on the process should reflect your changing needs, sometimes on a daily basis. Your energy must be focused on "the job at hand" so to speak. You will need to think differently when you are coordinating three different contractors to build a house than when you are doing all of the work yourself. If you write a book, the research requires a different concentration and different capabilities compared to the actual writing itself. The initial writing calls for a different focus than the editing and rewriting. For a long term project, most of the template may stay the same as different strategies are used at different times.

I quoted Tony Robbins in the Look Forward chapter as saying "Controlled focus is like a laser beam that can cut through anything that seems to be stopping you..." It has been my experience that I need to focus and refocus during the life of a project; sometimes on the big picture, sometimes on the task at hand.

Success is multidimensional; it has to do with your identity, what you believe in, your values, and your capabilities. When writing this book there were times when I needed to work on energy, times when I needed to remove interferences, and times when I needed to work on motivation and dedication. This process needs to be and is flexible; it brings a lot of things to you; you need to bring a lot of things to it.

Design a Template

You will design a template in the *Design Your Self-Evolutionary Template* chapter which is next. It is divided into the nine components with reference information for each given first. This is followed by instructions for filling out the Design Sheets in the *Design Sheets* chapter.

You will sketch out the nine components for the Self-Evolutionary process using pencil and paper. Depending on the component, you will answer questions, draw images, and describe internal dialogue and feelings

Implement the Template

You will implement the Self-Evolutionary template you create by embedding it into your conscious and unconscious awareness. You will embed each component of the Self-Evolutionary template, in the proper sequence, using spatial associations (spaces on the floor). You will do this by focusing on each spatial association, each piece of paper representing believe, decide, choose a strategy, etc. as you recreate the subjective experience (using the Design Sheets).

Use the Self-Evolutionary process for just about any task you want to perform. Since it is generic, it will support an almost endless list of tasks:

1. Recover from heart attacks, strokes, and other illnesses. It will help you see, feel, hear, taste, and smell determination to get well.

2. For behavior modification, to break or create habits, get a college education, or go straight home from work. Use it as a mastering tool.

3. For projects: write a book or an opera, build a house, change occupations. Not only will the Self-Evolutionary process help you design a project, embed it deep into your conscious and unconscious awareness, it will support you from milestone to milestone as you complete it.

4. To change beliefs, make decisions, develop strategies, change attitudes, program your day, or get a promotion. With time and experience, the Self-Evolutionary process will help you develop a successful personality.

5. To improve leadership qualities, have a more positive outlook,

and develop better relationships with self and others. The Self-Evolutionary process will teach you how to really believe, decide, make a commitment, and choose a strategy.

6. To help you establish a philosophy of life. The goal in this case could be a philosophy of life that improves your well being making you feel more comfortable and fulfilled. Strategies could be reading, going to philosophy classes, getting on a spiritual path or designing your own (spiritual path).

7. For skills like typing, reading, memory, studying, better concentration, computer programming, writing. The Self-Evolutionary process will teach you to get into a state of excellence to perform any task.

As a System

This process can be used to accomplish a task or a set of tasks. It can be used to accomplish a number of unrelated tasks or a number of related tasks that create a synergy, a gestalt, a comprehensive view of some part of your model of the world.

There are many ways of combining goals. One is free association. After performing a task you might think of another task that is related (logical relations, left brain) and would work well together (if integrated, right brain). After getting function back after a stroke someone might want to try a new craft to develop new motor coordination and thinking processes. Someone who learns to read faster might want to learn a new subject or even change careers. Someone who used the process to help recover from a heart attack, who found that combining beliefs, decisions, and strategies in this unique way, might want to take up golf as part of a program to stay in shape.

Another method for combining goals is to use formalized plans that others have set up and work well; matriculating at college, completing a correspondence course, updating your skills in a company sponsored program, learning a series of computer programs, or learning to program your VCR.

The Process Further Defined

Does it look like the Self-Evolutionary process is for you? The process is intended to be flexible, customize it as necessary.

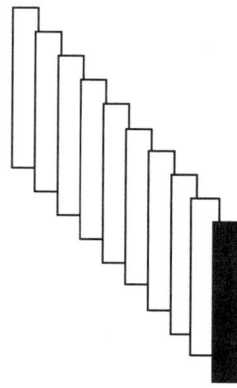

Design Your Self-Evolutionary Template

This chapter is divided into the nine Self-Evolutionary components. Background information for each is given along with instructions for filling out the Design Sheets. The Design Sheets are then used, along with the spatial associations, to install your plan for success into your conscious and unconscious awareness.

What is Reality?

What is actual, what is true? Your search for the reality of success is much closer to fruition. There are no guarantees in life but we have come a long way toward finding a template that you can use to schedule yourself for success. In the *Look Backward* chapter we got a look at how we developed the ability to perform temporal-sequential processes, to do things one step at a time. In the *Look Inward* chapter, we got a chance to see how we do most things unconsciously. Then in *Mental Tools,* we saw how we could create, enhance, associate, and then project subjective experience into the future to obtain a goal. This chapter is where *your* version of reality is the most important, where your subjective experience, which can only come from your reality, is used to create a template which programs you for success. What is reality? You are about to create it. Your reality for success.

It is time to create and record your subjective experience for each of the Self-Evolutionary components. Use a pencil, keep an eraser handy, along with extra copies of the Design Sheets.

> It is perfectly okay to rearrange the sequence of the Self-Evolutionary components if it makes you more successful.

The background information for each component listed below is accompanied by an expanding block diagram of a sample template, along with sample Design Sheets, to be used as models.

Entertain Ideas

We are human beings, we think! One of the most natural methods for entertaining a thought is to go through a question and answer routine until there are no more questions. If there are no more questions, there must be a belief, even if tentative. A belief can drive a decision and then a strategy of some sort.

Components

> Entertain Ideas

We have thousands of thoughts each day, one estimate is 60,000 thoughts during the waking state. Most happen routinely.

We have thoughts that surprise us, intrigue us, question us; some of them make demands. We search for ideas when we are solving a problem, bored with life, in pain, or have a desire for something different; *when we want to change our lives.*

The figure on page 89, shows one way of sorting ideas. If this model doesn't work well for you, create one that does; or modify this one. It isn't imperative for you to know how you decided to pursue an idea but it is of value to know more about how you think.

Use the figure as an example to fill out a **copy** of the Design Sheet for "Entertain an Idea" in the *Design Sheets* chapter on page 136.

The goal is to document how you came up with the idea. **This component is optional.**

Sample Design Sheet for "Entertain an Idea"

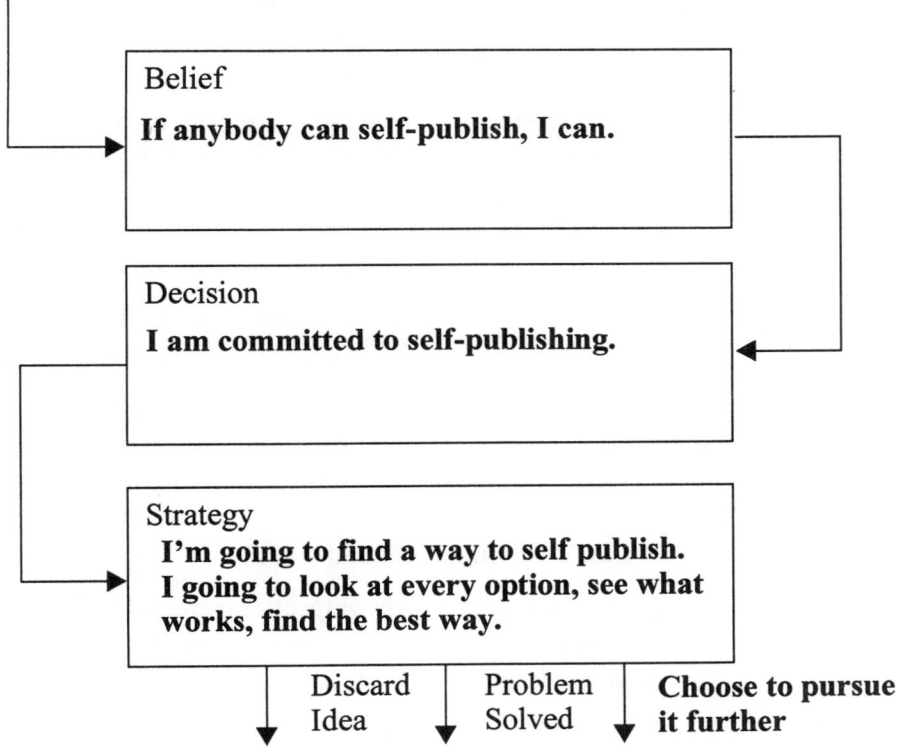

Originating Idea: **The book is finished, I want to self-publish it.**

Question: **How do I find out how to self-publish?**

Answer: **I'll look on the internet.**

Question: **How do I keep from being ripped off?**

Answer: **I'll trust my instincts and do some research.**

Question: **Can I really self-publish?**

Answer: **If anybody can self-publish, I can.**

Belief

If anybody can self-publish, I can.

Decision

I am committed to self-publishing.

Strategy

I'm going to find a way to self publish. I going to look at every option, see what works, find the best way.

Discard Idea   Problem Solved   **Choose to pursue it further**

Qualify an Idea

You have an idea you want to pursue. Is it a good idea?

Components

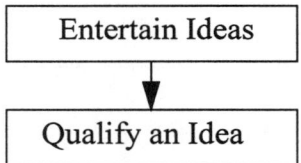

If you want to soar with eagles you need a preflight inspection and a good flight plan. This section is like a preflight inspection. You have an idea you want to pursue but you want to see if "it is going to fly" before investing resources. You want an idea you can believe in; a goal that is really good for you.

A Good Goal

How do we evaluate goals? A goal must give us something we need or desire without causing problems. Let's look at several ideas that can be used to evaluate goals.

1. The goal must be achieved in a secure manner. This is another way of saying that the goal will really give us what we want and what we want is really good for us. It does not affect life, family, business (job), or friends adversely. I believe that the goal should also be honest and fair to others.

2. If the idea you want to pursue contains a problem and your goal is a solution, you need to satisfy two things with your goal.

   Original intentions: if the present condition has an original intention, like smoking was originally intended to let you fit in with peers, find a way that the solution also lets you "fit in." The original intention needs to be satisfied. A former smoker might join a running club and fit in.

   Derived gains: if after developing the smoking habit it relaxed you (a derived gain) then the solution needs to relax you; if it is going to work well.

3. It must be initiated and maintained by you (of your own volition)

using resources you have or can obtain. It is also highly desirable to have the goal be something that you "want" to do rather than something you "must" do. If you have something that you must do and don't initially want to, change your belief. Find reasons to want to. You can use a template just for that.

4. It must be sensory based. Creating subjective experience and projecting it into the future is sensory based; all five senses plus language are used; each temporal-sequential step of the way.

5. It must be stated in positive terms. It must be stated in terms that explain what you want rather than what you don't want. Become "smoke free" rather than "stop smoking," for example.

In a Secure Manner

Consider how the goal will affect your life, family, friends, or business; if at all. If there are negative consequences, how can they be minimized or eliminated. Weigh the advantages and the disadvantages (on the one hand you get one thing and on the other hand...) or maybe this is a win/win situation.

Use the Design Sheet shown below as an example and then fill out a **copy** in the *Design Sheets* chapter on page 137. Use the sheets in the *Design Sheets* chapter as originals to make copies from so that you can protect them. It's also a good idea to keep the Design Sheets after you are through with them (perhaps a Self-Evolutionary Journal) so that you can refer back to them for analysis and planning new templates for new goals.

> You have the power and the stability of the universe supporting you. You have millions of years of genetic evolution in your gene pool. You are part of the gene pool that has created great art, charted the planets, and placed a telescope into space that can "almost" see to the edge of time.

Sample Design Sheet for "Qualify an Idea" Sheet 1

Q. What good will happen if you get the result?
A. I will be fulfilling my mission; succeeding and helping others to succeed.
Q. What bad, if anything, will happen? Consider this question carefully.
A. None that I can think of.

Q. What **good** will happen if you don't get it?
A. None that I can think of.

Q. What won't happen if you are successful?
A. I won't continue being unfulfilled.

Q. What do you get to have (or keep) by not having the goal?
A. Un-fulfillment.
Q. Is there a reason that you might be hesitant to obtain the goal?
A. I must take care not to overwork myself.

Q. When, where, and with whom does obtaining the goal work for you?
A. As soon a possible, in the best place, with good people.

Q. Is there any reason to believe that this idea will not work?
A. If my marketing strategy is poor, it may not work.

Q. How will the goal affect your complete system (family, friends, etc.)?
A. My family and friends will benefit when I am more successful.

Original Intentions/Derived Gains

Some people make the argument that there is an original intention for every behavior; it makes sense. If we don't have an intention we are without motivation. There is often problems associated with not having motivation.

Someone begins jogging to become healthier, he learns to like the "runner's high" very much but his knees begin to suffer. He then substitutes an exercise program that concentrates more on the upper body which is suitable for his knees and then he meditates with breathing exercises to substitute for the runner's high. Both the original intention and the derived gain are maintained.

Original intention: The motivation for a behavior.

Derived gains: Where a behavior carries out some positive function even though it is largely negative. Drinking allows some alcoholics to be sociable.

Remember to fill out a **copy** in the *Design Sheets* chapter on page 138.

Sample Design Sheet for "Qualify an Idea" Sheet 2

Q. Does the idea you are pursuing resolve a problem, and if so, what is the original intention and how can it be maintained?
A. It resolves the problem of being unfulfilled. The original intention was to play it safe. Being more successful makes me safer (in the long run) and maintains the original intention.

Q. If you intend to resolve a problem does it have a derived gain and how can it be maintained?
A. There doesn't seem to be a derived gain.

Of Your Own Volition

When we take responsibility for our lives we, by necessity, have to eliminate other people from being responsible.

Remember to fill out a **copy** in the *Design Sheets* chapter on page 138.

Sample Design Sheet for "Qualify an Idea" Sheet 3

> Q. Will the idea that you are pursuing be initiated and maintained by you?
> **A. Yes.**
>
> Q. Do you have the resources to carry out the idea or able to get them?
> **A. I need a loan and access to the marketplace.**

Sensory Based

Since we operate in life through the information obtained from our five senses, we can have confidence in processes that use images, feelings, sound, (smell and taste per your appetite). Creating subjective experience and projecting it into the future uses all of the sensory modalities.

Remember to fill out a **copy** in the *Design Sheets* chapter on page 138.

Sample Design Sheet for "Qualify an Idea" Sheet 4

How will you know when you are successful? What will you:
See: **Me selling books to people happy to get them.**
Hear: **The sound of people discussing the ideas in the book.**
Feel: **Excited and secure.**
Smell: **The sweet smell of success.**
Taste: **A special toast of congratulations.**

Using Positive Language

Use Positive language to state your goal. The power of language is in its ability to direct the brain. Negative language doesn't direct the brain very well; consider the following:

1. The brain, when it is instructed to, goes in a direction. It sees, hears, and feels messages and goes in a particular direction to fulfill the instructions. Have you ever told yourself that you were

going to the store to get something that you like; felt excited about going; saw yourself stopping for gas on the way; reminded yourself to negotiate on price as explained in the book you read on negotiating; visualized how you would approach the sales person; imagined the tone of voice you would use; winced and acted like you had been stabbed in the stomach when the sales person gave you the price; and you then gave a counter offer, lower in price. If you haven't done this, try it, you might find it fun. And when you wince at the price, really lay it on, they rehearse giving you the price, you can rehearse receiving it. Remember to give your brain direction when you want to do something.

2. The brain responds well to positive instructions and does **not** respond well to negative instructions. A negative is not a direction, at least not one the brain can follow easily. For example, when you are told **not** to do something, your brain usually sees you **do** it. Automatically. (Right now, if you tell yourself "**do not** see a blue elephant," what comes to mind; what is that subtle image that goes along with "do not see a blue elephant"?) A blue elephant, of course.

    We use negative language when we are speaking and it has its place but when we are giving instructions to ourselves or to others, avoid the negatives.

    The brain can't see you **not** doing something. What is the image of a boy **not** running through the park. There are an infinite number of possibilities, an infinite number of images of a boy not running through the park that the brain could generate, he could be "standing in the park," for instance. The brain cannot generate an infinite number of images, and if it could, it could not use an infinite number of images to go in a particular direction. What direction is infinity. Negatives have a minimal impact on the brain.

    Let's look at an example. The parent tells the child:

      "**Don't** run, you're going to fall down."

      The child falls down.

      "I told you so."

      "You **never** listen to me."

    Now, read the example above but skip the negatives shown in bold type.

Speak to yourself, speak to others in positive terms. The more specific the better. If you unintentionally use a negative, follow it with two positives. Rather than saying that you are going to stop procrastinating, say you are going to do things "on time."

Use the design sheets that follow as an example for using positive language. Some of the questions cover topics that we haven't discussed yet. Use them as an introduction of things to come; a preview of what the full process is like.

Remember to fill out a **copy** in the *Design Sheets* chapter on page 139.

Sample Design Sheet for "Qualify an Idea" Sheet 5

Q. Describe your goal in positive terms. **A. I am going to self-publish, successfully.**
Q. Describe why the goal is a good one and will not cause problems. **A. Self-publishing successfully gives me control; I can do it, I can see stacks of books, money in my checking account, people becoming more successful.**
Q. Describe your belief about the goal in positive terms. **A. Self-publishing works, if anyone can do it, I can do it.**
Q. Describe your decision (commitment) to pursue the goal in positive terms. **A. I have decided to self publish. I have made a firm commitment.**
Q. Describe your strategy to attain the goal in positive terms. **A. I am going to use Self-Evolutionary Templates and study publishing. I am going to market my book on my website.**
Q. Describe how you will project your goal into the future in positive terms. **A. I see books being sold, resources (money) growing, debts disappearing.**
Q. Describe how you will project the effects of your goal into the future. **A. I see a life with plenty of money and good health.**
Q. Describe the state of excellence you will use to perform successfully. **A. I see myself using this process each day. I see myself associating the whole process to my right ear lobe; I increase my belief and my excitement at will.**
Q. Describe how you will analyze the results of your effort. **A. I will take an inventory at the end of each day; what went well, what could have been better.**

Believe

You qualified an idea for a goal. Do you really believe in it?

Components

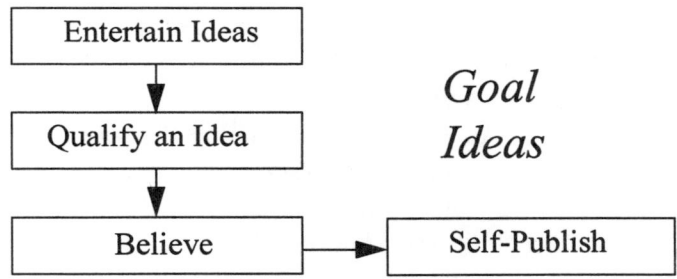

It is commonly thought that if we really believe that we can do something, we can. It is also said that: "faith moves mountains." Strengthening our belief about something strengthens our desire for it and helps to provide a sense of entitlement.

> If you are at a mental red light, belief can give you the green light.

Beliefs are important for the power that they contain but also because they affect decisions, strategies, indeed the whole Self-Evolutionary process.

I think that if there were no questions, there would be no beliefs. That thought might be somewhat philosophical and might have something of a chicken and egg flavor but certainly beliefs don't change unless they are questioned. If you have a belief, maybe someone else's belief originally, and it's not working for you, or circumstances have changed and it's "no longer" working for you, some type of questioning is necessary to arrive at another belief.

So the power of belief requires us to look at the other side of the coin. Wrong-headed beliefs can lead to disaster. In the 1980s the Soviet Union thought that the United States was getting ready for nuclear war. President Reagan made some careless remarks, the Soviet Union had a history of paranoia, and our intelligence people thought it was best to let them sweat it out, rather than to clarify the situation, at least initially. Ideas that have been thoroughly qualified are the best ones to pursue.

What are Beliefs?

We collect a myriad of beliefs as we live our lives: religious, spiritual, political, and professional. In 1969, the New York Mets won the World Series while proclaiming "you gotta believe." It is within that context that I am using the term "belief." Often we are taught **not** to believe in ourselves. Often parents and teachers find it necessary, for some reason, to teach kids that they are "not good enough" or "not smart enough." Some of us have limiting beliefs that last a lifetime through no intention of our own. And probably no intention on the part of the person who installed them for us.

Beliefs as used in this model are visions of the intended future. If it is true that questions lead to change, as I believe, then beliefs are the next step in the change process; a very powerful step.

It is perfectly okay to learn of a new way of doing something and want to try it. It is perfectly okay to really believe in it when you try it. It is perfectly okay for you to be successful using the new method, and if the idea doesn't work, it is perfectly okay to leave it behind and move on. You take the learnings with you but you leave behind ideas that don't work for you. It is then perfectly okay to find a better solution, really believe in it, and give it a good honest effort. This concept fits within the cybernetic model of using feedback as a control mechanism. There is no such thing as failure; only feedback.

A belief is not a strategy; it is not a "how to." It is not a behavior although it influences behavior. A belief is a general statement about two experiences or points of view.

1. A belief may be a general statement about cause.

   For example: "I can't type fast *because* I am a male and evolution has given the female better finger dexterity." My beliefs about typing can make a difference in how I type. A better belief is that "*since* a man held the world's record for typing for a number of years, men can type well, and I can type as good as I need to, and will."

2. A belief may also be a general statement about meaning. "Does difficulty in typing *mean* that I am a weak-willed failure?" No. I have a good character, I have been genetically designed to succeed, I succeed much more often than I fail, failure is only feedback for success; these things *mean* that I am a success becoming more successful.

3. Finally, a belief may be a general statement about limits. "A coworker told me that I would never be able to type fast." No. I have used a Self- Evolutionary template to become a fast, accurate typist. I have removed the *limits* in my thinking.

- View mistakes in relation to the pursuit of a goal so that they are instructive. Failure being viewed as feedback is how we learned to walk. All of those bumps, falls, jerks, and false starts are how we became bipedal, in this lifetime.

- Do not group, look at, or compare mistakes in relation to each other. This can cause a contorted view. You may come to believe that you only make mistakes and may become confused at to how the mistakes happened.

The following is how to empower a belief using a "reference belief." It is quick, easy, and powerful.

Use a Reference Belief

Do you consciously do things the way others do them? Modeling can be a great resource. I think that we are always looking for better ways of doing things and it's important to find good models. I believe we model ourselves more than anyone else. When we are doing something new, we naturally draw on our experience. Using a "reference belief" is a way of modeling ourselves; it's easy, here's how to do it.

Step 1. Evaluate the belief that you can obtain your goal.

Do this by checking your sensory experience (visual, auditory, feeling, etc.) using the instructions shown below. Be aware of as much as you can and remember that sensory experience can be subtle and yet powerful. If you are neurologically complete, you will have some image, feeling, or sound (internal dialogue) when you think of an idea. You only need to be aware of what you are seeing, feeling, and hearing in your mind. When you think about your "goal," what does it:

- look like?

- sound like?

- feel like?

- smell like, if any?

- taste like, if any?

- if it's a movie, how many sensory modalities are used?

Step 2. Choose a very strong belief that you presently have as a "reference belief."

It can be any belief that is strong. My favorite is that "I deserve to be the best that I can be."

Step 3. Evaluate the "reference belief" with the sensory modalities listed above.

Step 4. Make the "reference belief" as strong as possible by enhancing images, sounds, and feelings and any other method that works for you.

You might want to feel your reference belief "resonate throughout the universe" with reverberating sounds and glowing images.

Step 5. Associate (link) the "reference belief" to some part of your body that you usually do not use.

I always use my right ear lobe when I am using Self-Evolutionary Templates. Maintain the association as you perform the next step.

Step 6. Switch your attention back to your goal and make it as big and powerful as your reference belief; stronger if you like.

Strengthen images, sounds, feelings: what ever it takes to make your (goal) belief more powerful. It's okay to have a very large impact on your awareness.

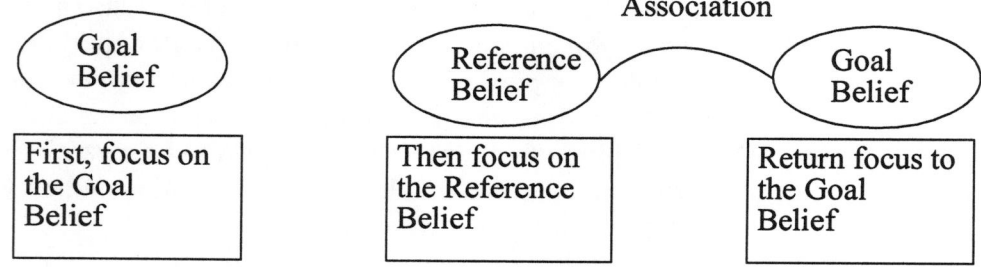

Step 7. **Release the association point knowing that you can regain the essence of the experience by firing off the association at any time.**

> I sometimes combine several beliefs to come up with my goal belief. I stack associations as described in the Mental Tools chapter.

Step 8. **Record the belief on a copy of the Design Sheet for "Believe" from the *Design Sheets* chapter on page 140.**

The goal is to have your belief associated well enough so that you can bring it back into your awareness when you implement the process in the *Implement Your Self-Evolutionary Template* chapter (next). Use the example shown below.

> You have the benefit of ancient wisdom; you have this process and the template you create with it but you alone can decide the kind of person you want to be, the kind of life that you want to live.

Sample Design Sheet for "Believe"

Visual image for Believe

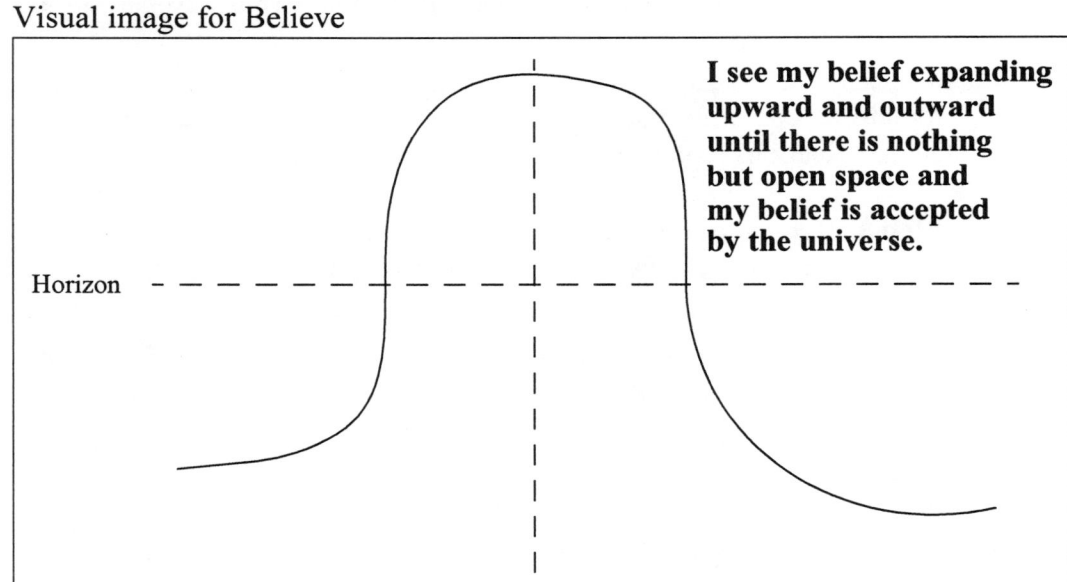

Horizon

I see my belief expanding
upward and outward
until there is nothing
but open space and
my belief is accepted
by the universe.

Left field of visualization | Right field of visualization

Internal Dialogue: I believe that I am entitled to be the best that I can be. I believe that I am going to successfully self-publish my book.

Feelings: I feel that I am stretching myself, life is not always secure. I sense the risk but there is also excitement and I know that I am doing a good job of working this out.

Decide

You believe in your goal but is there a better idea?

Components

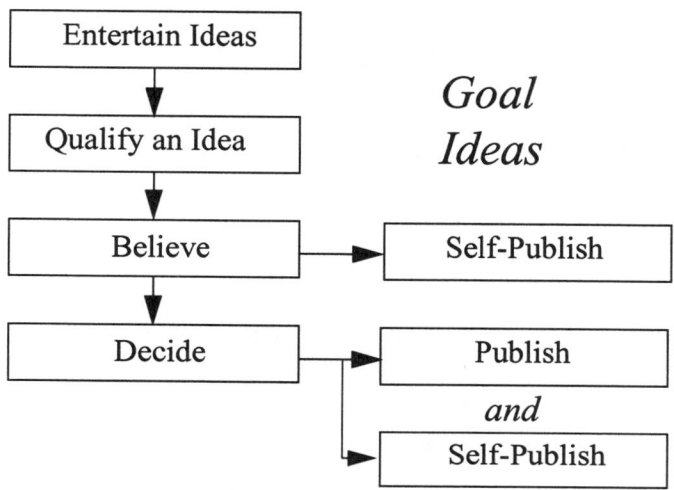

This decision process comes in two parts. First you will check to see if there are any better ideas and then, when the very best idea is secured, make a firm decision and a strong commitment.

Very often, a strong belief will drive a decision so strongly it seems unnecessary to even make the decision. If you listen to people's conversations you will sometimes hear a belief, decision, and strategy contained in one sentence. "I know the new models are really going to sell so I have decided to carry them in both lots and double the advertising." No matter how strong the belief is, it's important to make sure that the best idea available is being used. When that "sureness" has been established, make the decision and record it.

Decisions are commitments and it is necessary to make a firm commitment for a decision to be powerful. It is also important to remember that beliefs, decisions, and strategies affect one another. A strong belief can make a decision seem easy to make and a good strategy reinforces both the belief and the decision, indeed the whole process.

Decision Analysis

B.K. Skinner, a computer programmer and creator of the Gumption Trust, a trust designed to alleviate human suffering, has an interesting, simplified approach to decision analysis that can be used in everyday life: "Ask what the alternative courses of action are. Ask what the likely outcomes are. Decide what your relative preferences among the outcomes are."[1]

Lets put them into a numerical format.

1. Ask what the alternative courses of action are.

2. Ask what the likely outcomes are.

3. Decide what your relative preferences among the outcomes are.

You will be asked to weigh different goal ideas with numbers. The numbers are important even if you feel like you are guessing. "One of the main results of decision analysis research has been to show that a decision patched together with guesses and estimates is far better than no decision."[2]

You may investigate as many alternative options as you want; examples are given for three options (for my goal idea). My selections are circled in the following examples.

Use copies from the **Design Sheets** chapter on page 141.

Decision Analysis Work Sheet 1

Decide

↓

Goal idea **Self-publish my book.**	Likely outcome **I'll be better off in the long run because publishers usually don't promote books unless the author is well known.**

Does the goal fit in with your:

Identity_____   **Yes** (5) 4 3 2 1 0 1 2 3 4 5 **No**

Beliefs_____   **Yes** (5) 4 3 2 1 0 1 2 3 4 5 **No**

Values_____   **Yes** (5) 4 3 2 1 0 1 2 3 4 5 **No**

Capabilities_____   **Yes** 5 4 (3) 2 1 0 1 2 3 4 5 **No**

Long range goals_____   **Yes** 5 (4) 3 2 1 0 1 2 3 4 5 **No**

Short term goals_____   **Yes** 5 (4) 3 2 1 0 1 2 3 4 5 **No**

Other goals _____   **Yes** 5 4 (3) 2 1 0 1 2 3 4 5 **No**

Estimate the final score: **Yes** 5 (4) 3 2 1 0 1 2 3 4 5 **No**

Decision Analysis Work Sheet 2

Decide

↓

Goal idea **Find a publisher.**	Likely outcome **I will spend a lot of time learning how to find a publisher which might fail and even if I am successful, a book without promotion will probably fail.**

Does the goal fit in with your:

Identity_____ | **Yes** 5 4 3 2 1 0 1 2 (3) 4 5 **No**

Beliefs_____ | **Yes** 5 4 3 2 1 0 1 (2) 3 4 5 **No**

Values_____ | **Yes** 5 4 3 2 1 0 1 2 (3) 4 5 **No**

Capabilities_____ | **Yes** 5 4 3 2 1 0 1 2 (3) 4 5 **No**

Long range goals_____ | **Yes** 5 4 3 2 1 0 1 2 3 (4) 5 **No**

Short term goals_____ | **Yes** 5 4 3 2 1 0 1 (2) 3 4 5 **No**

Other goals _____ | **Yes** 5 4 3 2 1 0 1 (2) 3 4 5 **No**

Estimate the final score: **Yes** 5 4 3 2 1 0 1 2 (3) 4 5 **No**

Decision Analysis Work Sheet 3

Decide

Goal idea **Find a publisher who will let me self-publish while being published.**	Likely outcome **Selling a special edition of my book on on the internet will increase my chances for success in both markets. Seminars will also help both markets.**

Does the goal fit in with your:

Identity_____ **Yes** (5) 4 3 2 1 0 1 2 3 4 5 **No**

Beliefs_____ **Yes** (5) 4 3 2 1 0 1 2 3 4 5 **No**

Values_____ **Yes** (5) 4 3 2 1 0 1 2 3 4 5 **No**

Capabilities_____ **Yes** (5) 4 3 2 1 0 1 2 3 4 5 **No**

Long range goals_____ **Yes** (5) 4 3 2 1 0 1 2 3 4 5 **No**

Short term goals_____ **Yes** (5) 4 3 2 1 0 1 2 3 4 5 **No**

Other goals _____ **Yes** (5) 4 3 2 1 0 1 2 3 4 5 **No**

Estimate the final score: **Yes** (5) 4 3 2 1 0 1 2 3 4 5 **No**

Step 1. Use the numbers obtained to make your decision.

Then use the example of the Design Sheet for "Decide," shown below to fill out a copy in the *Design Sheets* chapter on page 142.

Step 2. Remember that approximations and estimates work very well to evaluate a particular goal idea.

Sample Design Sheet for "Decide"

Visual image for Decide

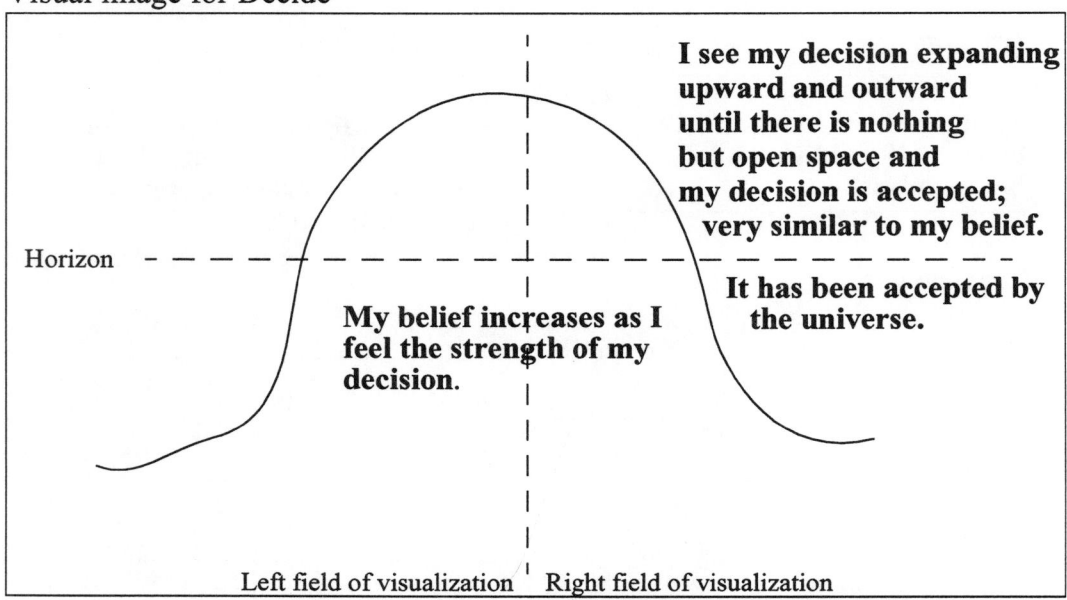

Internal Dialogue: I have decided and will pursue strongly, self publishing my book as well as publishing it in the traditional manner.

Feelings: I feel good internally, I know where I am going.

Choose a Strategy

You have made a good decision, what is the best strategy?

Components

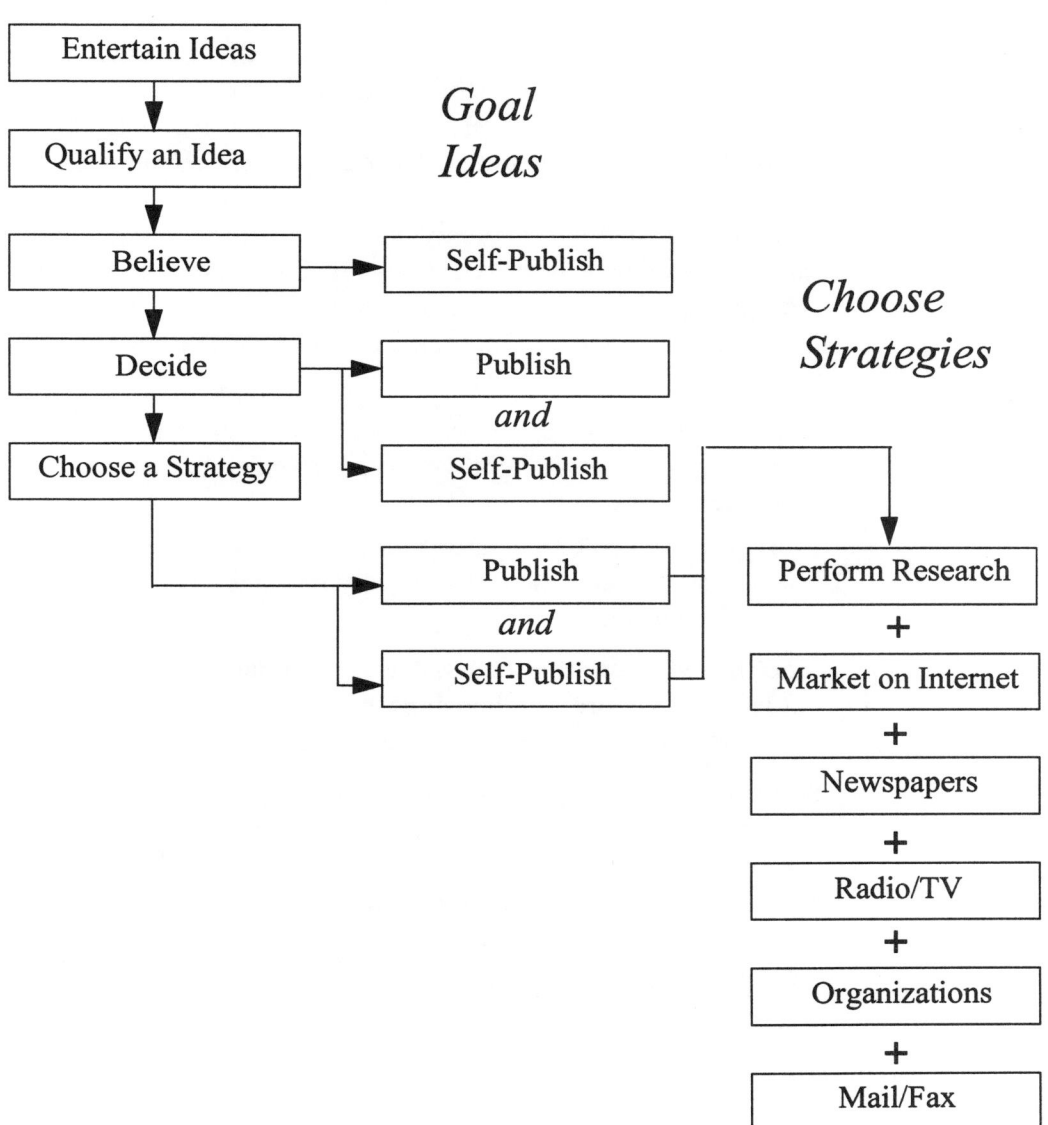

I watch the History Channel often. I enjoy it but I also like to study how different people in history have dealt with belief, decision, and strategy. John F. Kennedy made the decision to blockade Cuba during the Cuban Missile Crisis instead of invading the island as most of his top military advisors recommended. The military advisors didn't know that the

Russians had installed 42 or more (it depends on who counts them) tactical nuclear weapons in Cuba and were ready to use them if invaded. It is hard to imagine how World War III could have been avoided if tactical nuclear weapons had been used against the east coast of the United States.

JFK believed that an invasion of Cuba would have caused Khrushchev to react, probably by taking over Berlin if not beginning an all out war. He believed in a more moderate course of action and decided to use a blockade as part of a strategy to get Khrushchev to agree to remove the missiles. Another part of JFK's strategy was to be firm in his demand that the missiles be removed. It was JFK's firmness that caused Khrushchev to come to believe that he had misread JFK's personality, helped him to decide to back down and remove the missiles.

The more reference experiences we have, ours and other people's, the better insight we have for selecting and using strategies to obtain goals.

1. Since you are using this process, it is part of your strategy. At times it can be the entire strategy; if your goal is to change a belief, for instance.

2. Since this is a generic process, it doesn't contain strategies per se but has a procedure for choosing strategies. If it looks similar to Decision Analysis, choosing a strategy is a decision.

So have fun looking at a lot of different strategies. Evaluate them from different points of view. The more options the better and be sure to evaluate them well. In the example I have two goals: to "self-publish" and to "publish traditionally."

Make as many copies of the Strategy Analysis Work Sheet from the *Design Sheets* chapter on page 143 as you need.

Strategy Analysis Work Sheet

Choose a Strategy

Use as many work sheets as you need.

Strategy idea: **Self Publish.**	This procedure is a selection process but it is also a brain storming process. Use any technique that will give you a lot of strategy ideas to choose from.

List and rate ideas that might enable you to choose a strategy.

Make a list of resources on Internet_   **Yes** (5) 4 3 2 1 0 1 2 3 4 5 **No**

Perform research at the library_____   **Yes** 5 4 (3) 2 1 0 1 2 3 4 5 **No**

Check out book stores_____   **Yes** 5 (4) 3 2 1 0 1 2 3 4 5 **No**

Start my own publishing company__   **Yes** 5 4 3 (2) 1 0 1 2 3 4 5 **No**

Talk to successful writers_____   **Yes** (5) 4 3 2 1 0 1 2 3 4 5 **No**

Check for lists of organizations_____   **Yes** 5 (4) 3 2 1 0 1 2 3 4 5 **No**

Sell books on the street_____   **Yes** 5 (4) 3 2 1 0 1 2 3 4 5 **No**

Strategy Analysis Work Sheet

Choose a Strategy

Use as many work sheets as you need.

Goal idea: **Find Publisher**	This procedure is a selection process but it is also a brain storming process. Use any technique that will give you a lot of options to choose from.

List and rate ideas that might enable you to find and choose a strategy.

Make a list of resources on Internet_   **Yes** 5 4 ③ 2 1 0 1 2 3 4 5 **No**

Perform research at the library_____   **Yes** 5 ④ 3 2 1 0 1 2 3 4 5 **No**

Check out book stores_____   **Yes** 5 4 ③ 2 1 0 1 2 3 4 5 **No**

Start my own publishing company__   **Yes** 5 ④ 3 2 1 0 1 2 3 4 5 **No**

Talk to successful writers_____   **Yes** 5 ④ 3 2 1 0 1 2 3 4 5 **No**

Check for lists of organizations_____   **Yes** 5 4 3 ② 1 0 1 2 3 4 5 **No**

Sell books on the street_____   **Yes** 5 4 3 2 1 0 1 2 3 4 ⑤ **No**

Note: The example above for Find Publisher has the same resource categories as Self Publish but the individual resources will be different, with some overlap. A book on publishing might cover both self-publishing and being published, for instance.

Step 1. Use the example of the Design Sheet for "Choose a Strategy," shown below to fill out a copy in the *Design Sheets* chapter on page 144.

Step 2. Use the numbers from the work sheets to determine the best components for a strategy.

Sample Design Sheet for "Choose a Strategy"

Visual image for Choose a Strategy

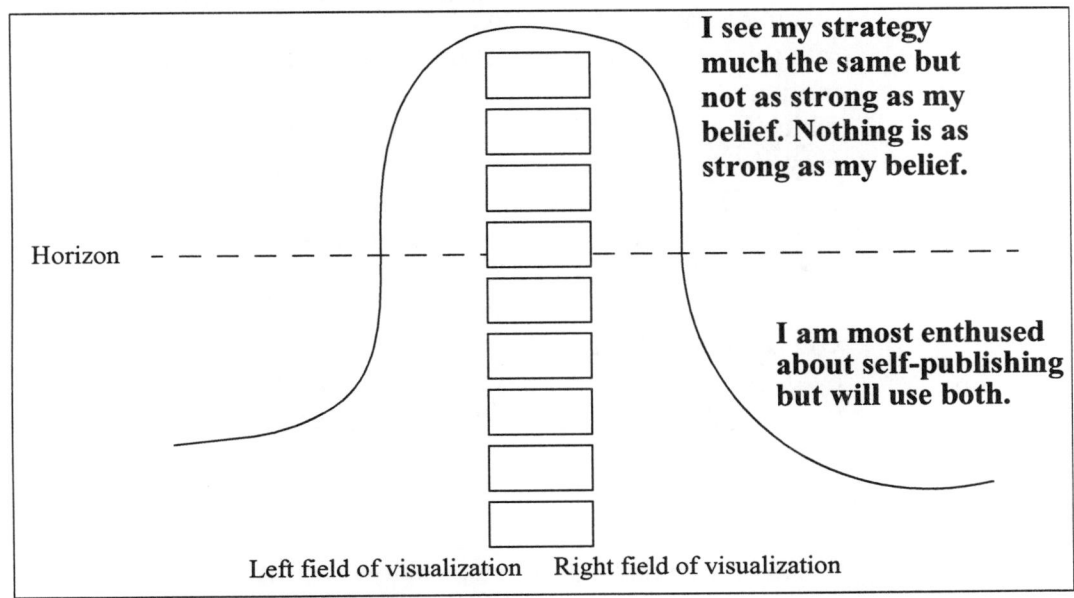

I see my strategy much the same but not as strong as my belief. Nothing is as strong as my belief.

I am most enthused about self-publishing but will use both.

Horizon

Left field of visualization   Right field of visualization

Internal Dialogue: I am going to research both ways of publishing. I am also going to market tapes and seminars.

Feelings: I feel anxious to get started.

> **Stop**: Go back and review the previous Design Sheets to see if any of the Self-Evolutionary components have changed.
> Beliefs, decisions, and strategies have a tendency to interact, if you change one the others might also change.

Project the Goal

Can you project the goal into the future in a compelling manner? The brain loves to take direction. Projecting your goal into the future gives your brain direction but also timing and motivation. You can project your goal using your time concept which is especially good if you have a deadline to meet. Or you may choose to project it into the future in a more general time frame. There are two ways of viewing the goal. One is from the "director's view" where you see yourself obtaining (or having obtained) the goal as if you were an onlooker. You are playing the "director" role. The other is from the "actor's view" where you see yourself in your own body, looking through your own eyes, as you obtain (or have) the goal. You are playing the "actor" role. Both are important. Both can be done as still shots or panoramic movies.

Director's View

When you go through the steps below you will first be asked to see the goal, in your mind, from the director's view. In some ways it is less powerful than the actor's view but more objective.

You will be asked to see yourself having the goal, saying good internal dialogue, and feeling good.

> I see myself on a morning television program, I have real good rapport with the host and the audience, I am confident and relaxed. I feel as if I am in the audience watching me, watching the whole production. I describe and demonstrate the book and am received very well and asked to come back. After it is over, after I end it, I clap and yell. This is a great moment in my life, a great moment in my mind. I am the director, I can do this as many times as I want.

If it's a movie, as in the example above, have the scene last long enough so that your brain is directed in a compelling manner. You are directing the scene, use sensory adjustments (change the images, sounds, and feelings to make them more compelling) and whatever else makes it REALLY COMPELLING.

Actor's View

When you go through the steps below you will be asked to see the goal, in your mind, from the actor's view, acting it out with authority. See, feel, and hear it through your own eyes. Make it very compelling.

> I am announced and walk onto the set. The audience is clapping and I look out and acknowledge them through the glare of the lights, then turn to the host. She is warm and encouraging and I feel her eyes nudging me on; I look at her and shake my head yes. I shake hands and sit down, anxious, excited, and relaxed just the way I projected it. I know that I am going to do well, I feel the support of the Self-Evolutionary template that I used this morning.

It's okay to switch back and forth between the actor's and director's view. You may have more feeling in the actor's view. You might want to go back to the director's view for an objective look and then adjust the details so that it becomes more compelling. When you have worked things out to your satisfaction, go back to the actor's view and act it out again. If you let yourself go you will be able to flip back and forth between views, get new ideas, and redo scenes with rushes of imagination and power.

This is your movie, make it compelling. If you are as good of an actor and director for the Self-Evolutionary process as you are when you daydream, you will do just fine. By the way, how do you direct your daydreams? I'm sure we all do it differently but with experimentation, we can learn how we direct our daydreams and improve them; within the Self-Evolutionary process as described in this book.

Make the Projection

Step 1. Create a scene in your mind, from the director's view, where you are obtaining or have obtained your goal.

You are the director. Put it in the proper place in the future using your time concept or a more general time frame like the next time someone is disrespectful to you.

- What does it look like?

- What does it sound like?

- What does it feel like?

- What does it smell like, if you choose to?

- What does it taste like, if you choose to?

- If it's a movie with many or all of the sensory modalities listed above, how can you make it more compelling?

Step 2. **Adjust any of the images, sounds, and feelings to see what makes it the most compelling; are you in a room or a giant stadium, for instance?**

Step 3. **Associate the experience.**

Step 4. **Change the scene in your mind to where you are obtaining or have obtained the goal while in the actor's view.**

It can be a static scene or a movie. See it through your eyes.

- Put it into the future using your time concept as appropriate.

- What does it look like?

- What does it sound like?

- What does it feel like?

- What does it smell like, if you choose to?

- What does it taste like, if you choose to?

- If it's a movie with many or all of the sensory modalities listed above, how can you make it more compelling?

Step 5. **Adjust any of the images, sounds, and feelings to see what makes it the most compelling.**

Step 6. **Associate the experience.**

Re-evaluate the Goal

One of the benefits of developing the ability to really project your goal with clarity is that you can then reevaluate it. If it isn't compelling enough, go back through the process and see where you can enhance it. If it's very compelling, compelling enough to suit you, congratulations!

Fill out a **copy** of the Design Sheet on page 145 for "Project the Goal."

Sample Design Sheet for "Project the Goal"

Visual image for Project the Goal

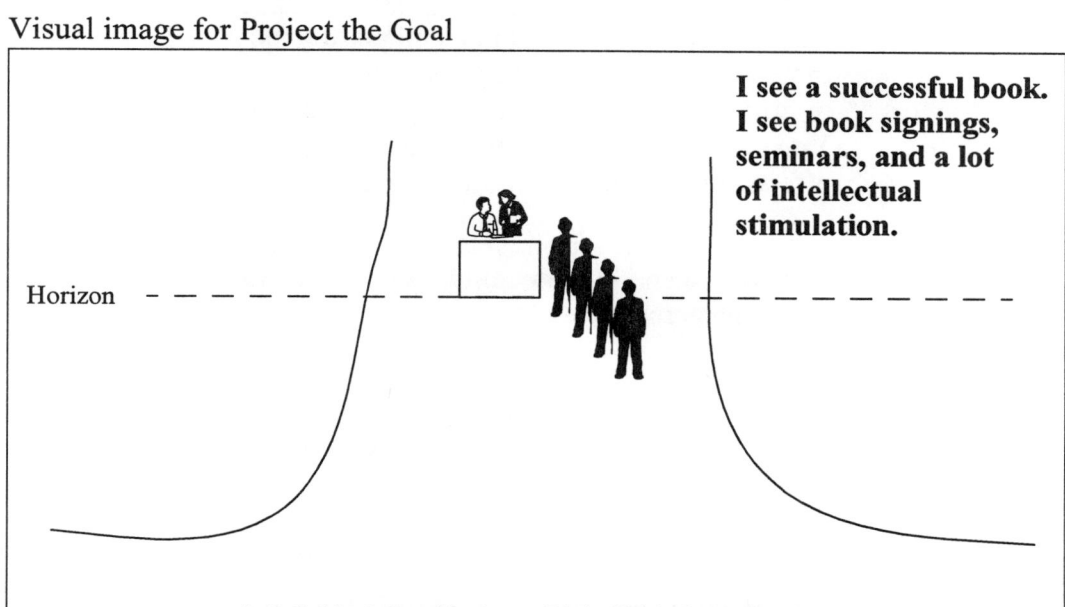

Horizon

I see a successful book. I see book signings, seminars, and a lot of intellectual stimulation.

Left field of visualization   Right field of visualization

Internal Dialogue: This is fun and fulfilling.

Feelings: Excited, each day is an exciting adventure.

Project the Effects

You can project the goal in a compelling manner, how about the effects? Projecting the effects into the future is very similar to projecting the goal; effects are generally more long term. You can use your time concept to be more exact or project the effects into a more general time frame.

Step 1. Create a scene in your mind where you can see the effects from the actor's view.

- What do they look like?

- What do they sound like?

- What do they feel like?

- What do they smell like, if you choose to?

- What do they taste like, if you choose to?

- If it's a movie with many or all of the sensory modalities listed above, how can you make it more compelling?

Step 2. Associate the experience.

Step 3. Change the scene in your mind to where you see the effects from the actor's view.

- What do they look like?

- What do they sound like?

- What do they feel like?

- What do they smell like, if you choose to?

- What do they taste like, if you choose to?

- If it's a movie with many or all of the sensory modalities listed above, how can you make it more compelling?

Step 4. Associate the experience.

Fill out a **copy** of the Design Sheet on page 146 for "Project the Effects."

Sample Design Sheet for "Project the Effects"

Visual image for Project the Effects

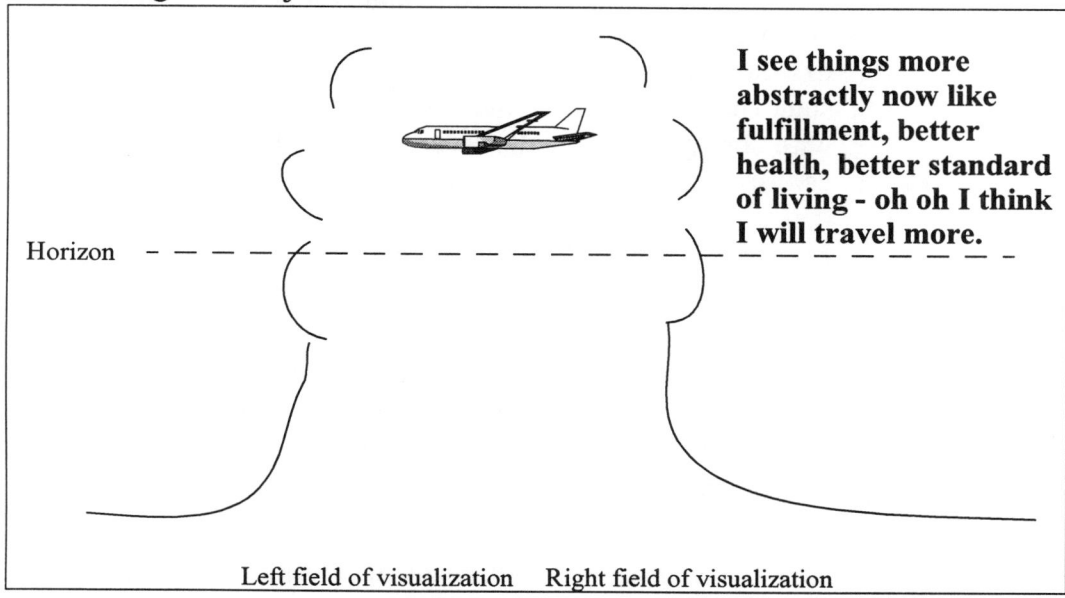

I see things more abstractly now like fulfillment, better health, better standard of living - oh oh I think I will travel more.

Horizon

Left field of visualization   Right field of visualization

Internal Dialogue: This is working better than expected. Once I learn more about marketing this is really going to take off.

Feelings: I'm surprised and excited. I have more options than I thought.

Perform Rehearsal

You have a great design, can you get into a state of excellence and perform it? This is where you develop a state of excellence, the state where you perform your best. This is the state you want to be in when you perform the task associated with your goal. You will associate (link) the state so that you can fire it off when needed. You may want to associate all of the subjective experience that you create for the Self-Evolutionary process, to the same point. Then, if you are working and need to refocus, fire off the association.

Important! I have a special Self-Evolutionary template that I designed to relax when I take time off. This is how I rejuvenate so that I am effective when pursuing my goals. I use my left ear lobe as an association point. I use the left ear lobe for relaxing; the right ear lobe for pursuing goals.

Important! It is also important to perform tasks that you schedule yourself for so that you are not all fired up and don't act on them. This can create stress. The key word for me concerning this issue is "balance."

Step 1. **Create a scene in your mind from the director's view where you see yourself performing a task, excellently.**

It might be the task that you are going to perform to obtain your goal. Or you might choose a reference experience where you were in a state of excellence in the past. I often use the experience of publishing four poems when I was in college. I really got excited.

- What do you look like?

- What do you sound like?

- Imagine what you feel like?

- Imagine what you might be smelling, if you choose to?

- Imagine what you might be tasting, if you choose to?

- If it's a movie with many or all of the sensory modalities listed above, how can you make it more powerful, dynamic, energetic?

Step 2. Associate the experience.

Step 3. Change the scene in your mind to where you are performing the task while in the actor's view (see it through your eyes).

- What do you see?

- What do you hear?

- What do you feel. What is the highest state of excellence you have ever felt?

- Imagine what you might be smelling, if you choose to?

- Imagine what you might be tasting, if you choose to?

- If it's a movie with many or all of the sensory modalities listed above, how can you make it more powerful, dynamic, energetic?

Step 4. Associate the experience.

Fill out a **copy** of the Design Sheet on page 147 for "Perform Rehearsal."

Sample Design Sheet for "Perform Rehearsal"

Visual image for Perform

Horizon

I see myself as a mental athlete; able to get into states of excellence at will. I have an association for up time and one for down time.

Left field of visualization   Right field of visualization

Internal Dialogue: I know that I can do this. I have programmed this so well, so many times, it is almost guaranteed.

Feelings: The highest state of excellence I have ever felt is associated with my right ear lobe. I know what I am doing and I am doing it well. I know where I am going.

Analyze the Results

You've done good, can you do it even better? One reason to analyze the results is to do better the next time, if it's that type of endeavor. Another reason is so that it's a more complete learning experience; a more complete learning experience makes a better reference experience for future use.

It is also human nature to want to know how well we did. We sometimes have a tendency to want to forget failures but that is like throwing away a reward that you worked for. The next time you see a very competitive sporting event and at the end the victors are jubilant and the losers are silent and downcast, try to guess which group is learning the most; which group is getting the most feedback. If you win or lose, get as much feedback as possible.

Repetition Counts

And of course there are times when repetition is the key to success. With a golf swing you might want to keep everything pretty much the same, after the beliefs and decisions are taken care of. You may want to try a number of strategies until you find the right one.

You might want to go back and remember a day when you were striking the ball beautifully, how you swung, what the golf club felt like as it moved into the ball, how you were able to keep your eye on the ball, what you were thinking at the time. You might want to hit the ball as you exhale, for instance. Would you associate these resources with the bottom of your feet, to your waggle, or to your exhale of breath? Experiment. Add confidence by remembering what it looked like, felt like, and sounded like to be confident some time in the past (it doesn't have to be about golf) and associate that memory with your swing or the bottoms of your feet. And remember to do it both in the actor state and the director state. It's an idea, keep it in mind when you play golf or practice at the driving range.

Fill out a **copy** of the Design Sheet on page 148 for "Analyze Results."

Sample Design Sheet for "Analyze Results"

Visual image for Analyze the Results

```
Horizon  - - - - - - - - - - - +    I don't have an image for this one.
                               |     And I don't analyze at a particular
                               |     time. I am very reflective and
                               |     analyze a lot but have difficulty
                               |     explaining how I do it which means
                               |     to me that a large component of it
                               |     must be unconscious.
                               |
                               |
                               |
                               |
                               |
                               |
                               |
                               |
         Left field of visualization | Right field of visualization
```

Internal Dialogue: I am going to analyze the results every evening before I go to sleep and embed the Self-Evolutionary process in my dreams.

Feelings: I feel like this is a complete, successful process that I can use for the rest of my life.

The Rubber Meets the Road

Having explained Self-Evolutionary Template design, I would like to say that a temporal-sequential process happens in a sequence, but the sequence doesn't necessarily have to be a seamless, orderly sequence. A Self-Evolutionary template can be used for a complex project where the process needs to be performed a number of times, in different circumstances, while focusing on different aspects of the project.

Something unexpected happens

When using the Self-Evolutionary process for a complex project; when the idea is well qualified, a powerful belief is maintained, with a good decision and a great strategy, this can all change when something unexpected happens. If you are planning a retirement account and congress passes a new law with better options for retirement accounts, you will want to take advantage of them if they apply to your situation. If you are building a house and one of the contractors goes bankrupt and doesn't fulfill his or her obligation, you will have to make adjustments and recover as much as possible.

A great strategy that was carefully chosen can begin to be doubted when circumstance underpinning the strategy change. If the strategy becomes doubtful then the decision and the belief are questioned and it is easy to have second thoughts.

There are no guarantees

We can most often work things out to minimize risks and have contingency plans if the whole process was well thought out. The ability to deal with complex projects with many contingencies is what makes us human; what differentiates us from the primates. There are no guarantees that success will always be easy and it becomes readily apparent to me that we developed big brains because we need them. It is also readily apparent to me that a well thought out plan for success increases our odds for success, greatly.

Sometimes, we even need to fail so that we can get the feedback to succeed next time. "Let's try it and see what happens." This makes succeeding the first time such a sweet spot.

Keep your finger on the pulse

These complexities reaffirm for me the role that questions play in the success process. When things are running smoothly there are few if any questions. When circumstances change, a new and better strategy may be needed with the rest of the process staying intact (and focus being maintained). This is why we, with larger more complex goals, need to keep our fingers on the pulse while at the same time keeping track of the big picture. I use this process every morning. Sometimes I use the process for the big picture and then immediately use it again for the particular part of the project that I am working on. This keeps me focused.

Making things too complicated?

We like quick easy answers but they can be very costly if we keep trying quick fixes that don't solve the problem or worse yet, make a blunder. I once had a writing assignment and used a technique that I had learned to solve a problem that had been around, in this particular company, for a number of years. The manager that I was working for was about to make a bad decision in an effort to solve the problem. I laid the whole problem out in an intelligent manner, showed three different options, and what the results were likely to be for each; and why. I wrote it up in a 50 page document that was used to make a good decision and most everybody was happy. My manager was happy, he avoided a mistake. So everything worked out well but guess what? I got the reputation among some of making things too complicated.

We do like quick, easy solutions and there is no doubt that they are great, when we can use them. But we sometimes have to look for better options, change strategies, crank up our beliefs, and refocus our energies. Reworking your Self-Evolutionary template for a particular project, as many times as is necessary, in an intelligent manner, is what will see you through if you desire a really difficult goal.

Reality Score Card

What is actual, what is true? We've seen it all. Does it look like this process is for you? The process is intended to be flexible, customize it as necessary. The goal is to get it to work for you. Let's go to the next chapter and implement your Self-Evolutionary template.

Endnotes

1. B.K. Skinner, *The Gumption Memo: Decision Making Techniques* (http://www.gumption.org).

2. Ibid.

If it is possible for anyone, it is possible for you.

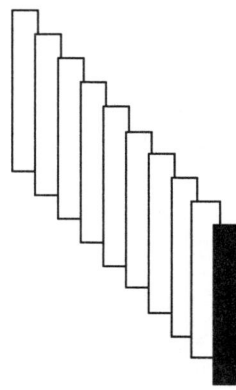

Implement Your Self-Evolutionary Template

You have created your Self-Evolutionary template; your reality for success. Because we are unable to hold all nine components of a template in short-term memory, at the same time, we have to embed them; we have to fix them in memory; securely, so that they will be available intuitively, instinctively, unconsciously. This is the way that we ride bicycles, make speeches, drive cars; how we perform tasks successfully. Embedding a template deeply in your memory programs you to obtain a particular goal but it also programs you to be more successful in the future. The more successful experiences you have in your life, the easier it is for you to be successful. This process can help you have a more successful personality.

We have a 5 to 10 million year history of doing things sequentially. How many times have you heard "Let's take this one step at a time?" You have already designed your template so it's just a matter of recreating your subjective reality while using spatial associations (to embed it in your brain in your skull) and also the brain (in your body); one step at a time.

Balance

Is life a balancing act? I believe that everything that I have investigated in my life can be out of balance including love, sidewalks, politics, and success strategies. It also seems to me that they can be out of balance at either end of the spectrum. Too much love can be suffocating while not enough robs us of our humanity.

I would like to caution against continually pumping yourself up for success without discharging the energy created, in a constructive manner (pursuing your goal). I have added layer on layer of beliefs, layer on layer of goals to be accomplished without doing enough to accomplish them and felt a lot of stress because of it.

I was coiling the spring, building up the motivation, and not releasing the energy by pursuing my goals. I was creating tension, stress, pressure, strain; what ever word you prefer. I then began to schedule my work time and down time with better balance. I began to enjoy that deep feeling of satisfaction when I am challenged and perform well; the joy of completing a task to my satisfaction. I also began to obtain and enjoy relaxation more.

Stress is not the same for everybody. One person's stress may be motivation for someone else. Only you can decide what stress is "for you" and how best to deal with it. If projecting a goal into the future causes you stress, you might consider making stress reduction a goal. It may require changing your environment (a quieter office), setting priorities, and achieving simpler goals first. It could also be that you are asking yourself to do something that you don't want to do, feel entitled to do, or feel incapable of doing.

Another consideration is that the "seeming" absence of symptoms does not guarantee the absence of stress. Medication, alcohol, drugs, and overeating may camouflage stress causing you to miss its signals and not reduce the strain on your physical and psychological systems.

Also, minor symptoms, such as headaches or stomach acid, may be stress symptoms. Minor symptoms of stress are the early warnings that you may be getting out of balance and need to do a better job of managing the activities in your life.

When I put things off, I often make the job larger (in my mind) than it actually is. This can be stressful, especially when I dwell on the things I haven't finished. I am at my best when I perform tasks without thinking about them, without making them a big deal (save the ones that need special attention).

Stress can be an issue in obtaining a "good goal" as described in the previous chapter, *Design Your Self-Evolutionary Template*.

Designing a Self-Evolutionary template and using it to achieve a goal can be a great stress reducer and fulfillment enhancer.

The Implementation Process

This process is used differently depending on whether the goal is a one-time event or a continuing project (proposing to your future wife or designing sky scrapers for a living). If you are accomplishing something over a period of time you should continually analyze your progress to determine how your goal is evolving and what needs to be done to further your objectives.

You may want to:

- perform the process before going to work each day, after you get home, or before you go to the university or fire house.

- fire off an association at different times during the day to maintain focus.

- just walk through the spatial associations (placed on the floor) without thinking and feel the focus. This works like magic for me after the template is established. My unconscious knows what is involved and aligns itself automatically.

State of Mind

This process can be performed in meditation, trance, or straight up. I have used trance a lot when working with myself and recently came to believe that I can tell myself anything "out of trance" that I can tell myself "in trace." It took a while for me to come to that conclusion. You will have to choose what is best for you. Experiment. A relaxed state might be the best way to begin.

Self-Evolutionary Components

The nine components (plus the reference component) are contained in the Spatial Associations chapter. The order that I have put the components in are what seems like the most natural; it has a logical resonance for me. If a different order works best for you, please feel free to change it. Different circumstances require different approaches. You might want to Choose a Strategy and feel comfortable with it before you Believe and Decide, for instance.

Implementing a Template

Implementing a template is the way that you schedule yourself for success. This is **not** where you perform the task, this is where you "program yourself" to perform the task. You may implement the template in several ways. You may:

1. Stand on each spatial association while looking at the appropriate Design Sheet to recreate the subjective experience. (This is usually best.)

2. Stand on each spatial association while someone reads the appropriate Design Sheet to you.

3. Use your memory to recreate what is on each Design Sheet.

4. Sit or stand at a distance imagining that you are at each spatial association as you review the Design Sheets.

It's more powerful to actually move from spatial association to spatial association, this gives your brain better direction. And of course, if you pull powerful feelings from the depths of your soul and bring them up to accompany the vivid images and potent internal dialogue, its okay. If you shake the universe, it's okay.

When circumstance change, you may have to change strategies. It's best to check or redo the whole template when one part changes.

The graphic below shows changing a strategy and then beginning again at *Qualify an Idea*.

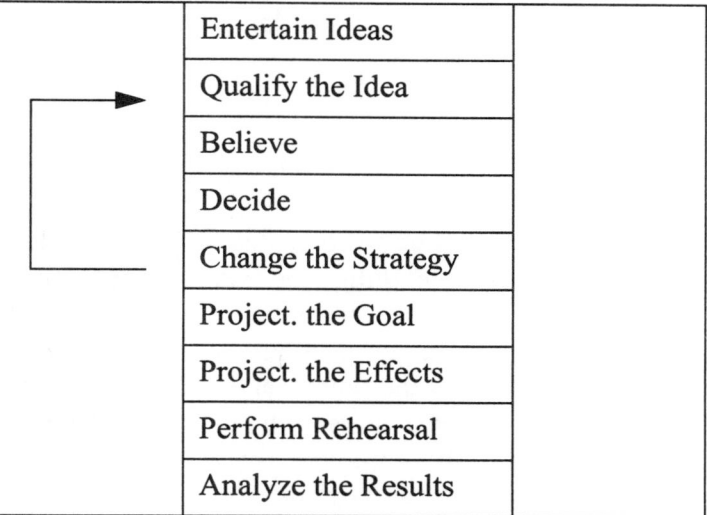

	Entertain Ideas	
	Qualify the Idea	
	Believe	
	Decide	
	Change the Strategy	
	Project. the Goal	
	Project. the Effects	
	Perform Rehearsal	
	Analyze the Results	

When implementing a template, I use the same association point that I use for the reference belief (right ear lobe) for each of the other components of the template. This strengthens the template and makes my right ear lobe my association for the Perform Rehearsal component. It also gives me an association to fire off when I need focus during the day.

I am very reflective and seem to always be analyzing something. I meditate in the morning, do some spiritual things, and then take an inventory of what I am thinking and feeling. This is when I address whatever template I am working on, analyze results, and decide what I am going to do that day. I also take a bedtime inventory of the events that happened during the day.

Reality Score Card

You have discovered your success reality and now have the opportunity to test it; the "proof is in the performing," so to speak. I think that reality is relative. Your reality will be altered to some degree after you have designed and implemented your first template and put it to use. Converting subjective reality into accomplishment causes you to change. I believe that we are always changing, its called learning, its called evolution, its called being human.

133

What is actual, what is true? The final test for your reality is whether or not you can obtain the goals you want. You have prepared well, go out and obtain your goal, claim your reward, and enhance your self-esteem. Park yourself in the winner's circle and stay there.

Epilog

Emotions can vary from day to day and anytime you do something new there is a potential for uncertainty in your mind. Uncertainty allows for change; this is especially true if you pursue a large success. This process is designed to smooth out the bumps and keep you focused. Be good to yourself and get technical and emotional support from all quarters. Besides obtaining a goal you are creating a reference experience that helps to define who you are, what you believe in, your values, and your capabilities. Your conscious and unconscious relies on reference experiences for future endeavors. Setbacks are temporary and success is to be enjoyed for the rest of your life. Watch other people's achievements and model them, especially their emotions as they earn and receive a gold medal in the Olympics or receive a Noble prize. You have your own Olympics and medals are in order when ever you go the distance. Be good to yourself.

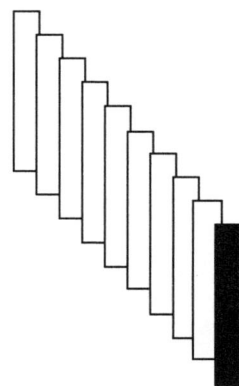

Design Sheets

Use the design sheets shown below to record the subjective experience you generate as you design your Self-Evolutionary template.

Design Sheet for "Entertain an Idea" (see page 89)

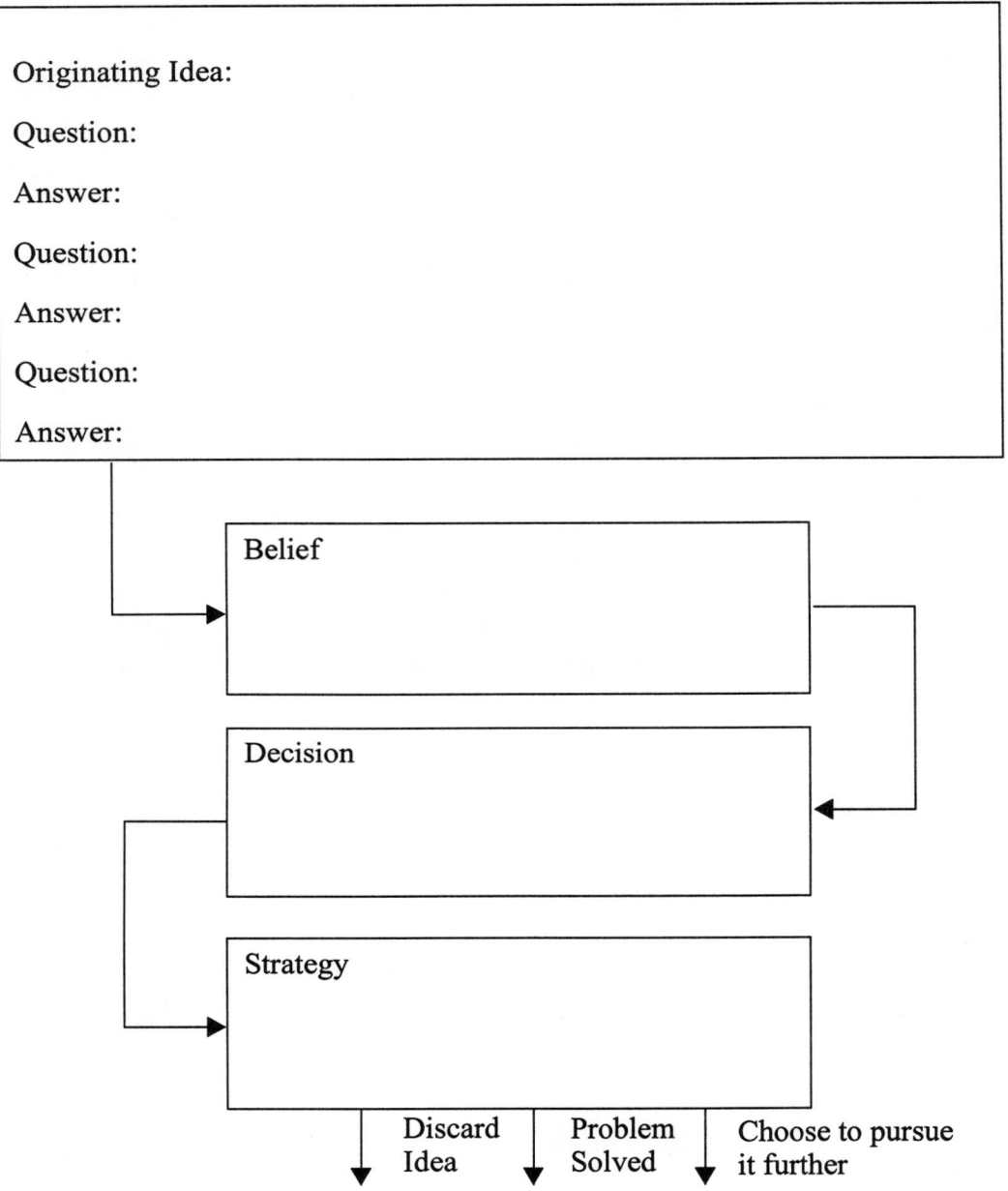

Originating Idea:

Question:

Answer:

Question:

Answer:

Question:

Answer:

Belief

Decision

Strategy

Discard Idea   Problem Solved   Choose to pursue it further

Design Sheet for "Qualify an Idea" Sheet 1(see page 92)

Q. What good will happen if you get the result?
A.
Q. What bad, if anything, will happen? Consider this question carefully.
A.

Q. What good will happen if you don't get it?
A.

Q. What won't happen if you are successful?
A.

Q. What do you get to have (or keep) by not having the problem?
A.

Q. Is there a reason that you might be hesitant to obtain the goal?
A.

Q. When, where, and with whom does having the goal work for you?
A.

Q. Is there any reason to believe that this idea will not work?
A.

Q. How will the goal affect your complete system (family, friends, etc.)?
A.

Design Sheet for "Qualify an Idea" Sheet 2 (see page 93)

Q. Does the idea you are pursuing resolve a problem, and if so, what is the original intention, and how can it be maintained?
A.

Q. If you intend to resolve a problem does it have a derived gain and how can it be maintained?
A.

Design Sheet for "Qualify an Idea" Sheet 3 (see page 94)

Q. Will the idea that you are pursuing be initiated and maintained by you?
A.

Q. Do you have the resources to carry out the idea or able to get them?
A.

Design Sheet for "Qualify an Idea" Sheet 4 (see page 94)

How will you know when you are successful? What will you:
See:
Hear:
Feel:
Smell:
Taste:

Design Sheet for "Qualify an Idea" Sheet 5 (see page 96)

Q. Describe your goal in positive terms. **A.**
Q. Describe why the goal is a good one and will not cause problems. **A.**
Q. Describe the belief about your goal in positive terms. **A.**
Q. Describe your decision (commitment) to pursue your goal in positive terms. **A.**
Q. Describe your strategy to attain your goal in positive terms. **A.**
Q. Describe how you will project your goal into the future in positive terms. **A.**
Q. Describe how you will project the effects of your goal into the future. **A.**
Q. Describe the state of excellence you will use to perform successfully. **A.**
Q. Describe how you will analyze the results of your effort. **A.**

Design Sheet for "Believe" (see page 102)

Visual image for Believe

```
Horizon  — — — — — — — — — — — — — — — — — — —

              Left field of visualization | Right field of visualization
```

Internal Dialogue:

Feelings:

Decision Analysis Work Sheet (see page 105)

Decide

Use as many worksheets as you need.

Goal idea

Likely outcome

Does the goal idea fit in with your:

Identity_____   Yes 5 4 3 2 1 0 1 2 3 4 5 No

Beliefs_____   Yes 5 4 3 2 1 0 1 2 3 4 5 No

Values_____   Yes 5 4 3 2 1 0 1 2 3 4 5 No

Capabilities_____   Yes 5 4 3 2 1 0 1 2 3 4 5 No

Long range goals_____   Yes 5 4 3 2 1 0 1 2 3 4 5 No

Short term goals_____   Yes 5 4 3 2 1 0 1 2 3 4 5 No

Other goals and desired outcomes___   Yes 5 4 3 2 1 0 1 2 3 4 5 No

Estimate the final score: Yes 5 4 3 2 1 0 1 2 3 4 5 No

Design Sheet for "Decide" (see page 108)

Visual image for Decide

```
                              |
                              |
                              |
                              |
                              |
                              |
  Horizon  - - - - - - - - - -+- - - - - - - - - - - -
                              |
                              |
                              |
                              |
                              |
                              |
            Left field of visualization | Right field of visualization
```

Internal Dialogue:

Feelings:

Strategy Analysis Work Sheet (see page 111)

Choose a Strategy

Use as many work sheets as you need.

↓

Strategy idea:	This procedure is a selection process but it is also a brain storming process. Use any technique that will give you a lot of strategy ideas to choose from.

List and rate ideas that might enable you to choose a strategy.

_____ | **Yes** 5 4 3 2 1 0 1 2 3 4 5 **No** |

_____ | **Yes** 5 4 3 2 1 0 1 2 3 4 5 **No** |

_____ | **Yes** 5 4 3 2 1 0 1 2 3 4 5 **No** |

_____ | **Yes** 5 4 3 2 1 0 1 2 3 4 5 **No** |

_____ | **Yes** 5 4 3 2 1 0 1 2 3 4 5 **No** |

_____ | **Yes** 5 4 3 2 1 0 1 2 3 4 5 **No** |

_____ | **Yes** 5 4 3 2 1 0 1 2 3 4 5 **No** |

Design Sheet for "Choose a Strategy" (see page 113)

Visual image for Choose a Strategy

Horizon

Left field of visualization | Right field of visualization

Internal Dialogue:

Feelings:

Design Sheet for "Project the Goal" (see page 117)

Visual image for Project the Goal (Would you like to draw your time concept?)

Horizon

Left field of visualization | Right field of visualization

Internal Dialogue:

Feelings:

Design Sheet for "Project the Effects" (see page 119)

Visual image for Project the Effects

Horizon –

Left field of visualization | Right field of visualization

Internal Dialogue:

Feelings:

Design Sheet for "Perform Rehearsal" (see page 122)

Visual image for Perform

```
                                    |
                                    |
                                    |
                                    |
                                    |
Horizon  – – – – – – – – – – – – – –|– – – – – – – – – – – – – – – –
                                    |
                                    |
                                    |
                                    |
                                    |
                                    |
                                    |
             Left field of visualization | Right field of visualization
```

Internal Dialogue:

Feelings:

Design Sheet for "Analyze Results" (see page 124)

Visual image for Analyze the Results

Horizon	
Left field of visualization	Right field of visualization

Internal Dialogue:

Feelings:

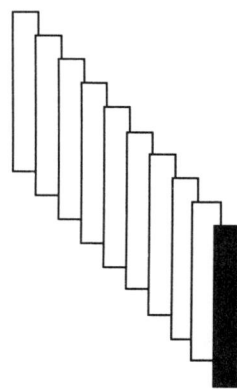

Spatial Associations

The sheets in this chapter are used to link the Self-Evolutionary template components into your memory (the memory in your brain and the memory in your body) in the proper sequence. Since they are used on the floor you might consider having a set of them laminated. You could have this done for you at your local printer or one of the major chain stationary stores (Office Depot, Staples, OfficeMax etc.). The Resource association is not one of the regular components. It is a resource to be used as a "model" for a belief, decision, strategy, etc.

Resource

Entertain

Ideas

Qualify an

Idea

Believe

Decide

Choose a Strategy

Project the

Outcome

Project the Effects

Perform

Rehearsal

Analyze

SET for Success is a mastering tool. Use it to get well, get promoted, get educated, change careers, or any other goal you want to obtain.

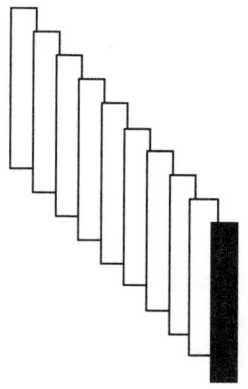

Summary

The following summary is by chapter.

Look Forward

We all have different views of reality with different ideas of what success is and how to obtain it. The philosophy of this book is that we, by necessity, have to decide what success is for ourselves and how to obtain it in a manner consistent with our view of reality. You are invited to use this book not only to find out what your "reality for success" is but to design and implement Self-Evolutionary templates which will help you to obtain goals consistent with your "view of reality."

Look Backward

This chapter takes a look at human evolution and observes that temporal-sequential processes in the human brain supported walking a step at a time, speaking a word at a time, performing tasks a step at a time from fashioning flint tools to performing operations in math. The implication is that a process for programming success should be performed in a temporal-sequential manner, one step at a time. This chapter also tells us how we use five senses plus language to get on with our lives.

Note: Language predominates our "linguistic" thinking but language cannot exist without the five senses.

Look Inward

This chapter looks at what consciousness is, how we learn and think, and comes to the conclusion that most of our learning and thinking is done in an unconscious manner. We are aware of some of the things going on when we learn but there is even more going on behind the scenes. The same is true with our thinking.

If we stopped to think about each thing we did, consciously, we could get very little done. Since we learn, think, and perform in an unconscious manner, for the most part, a plan for success needs to be embedded both in our conscious and unconscious awareness. The Self-Evolutionary process uses spatial associations to accomplish this.

Mental Tools

This chapter describes creating, enhancing, and associating subjective experience to flesh out our visions and desires for success. The way that we envision (see, hear, and feel) our next project determines the resolve we will bring to it.

A large component of life is the way that we divide time and space with our thoughts and actions. When we jog, drive to work, play golf, or manage a business we are dividing time and space. The words we speak come out one at a time (time) and take up space (the air that we vibrate with our vocal chords).

We are dividing time and space when we sequence our sensory systems (visual, auditory, feeling, smell, and taste; also called sensory modalities) as we think. These are the raw ingredients for subjective experience which give us control over our thoughts and actions.

We can enhance our subjective experience using sensory adjustments (adjust visual, auditory, feeling, smell, and taste experiences). Sensory adjustment is a powerful tool but only one of many tools we have to obtain goals and create our future.

Directions are given for enhancing feelings, generating strong images that are clear and bright, and creating good internal dialogue that resonates with power. And of course, one of the reasons to create, enhance, and associate subjective experience is so that we can project it into the future (to schedule us for success). This can be done intuitively or with the time concept that we have inside of our minds.

Overview

Subjective experience (five senses plus language) is created and enhanced for each of the components needed for success. The subjective experience is implemented (embedded in the brain) and projected into the future as you schedule yourself for success. This is accomplished within the process of designing and implementing Self-Evolutionary templates.

Design Your Self-Evolutionary Template

Subjective experience is created and enhanced for each of the components needed for success (believe, decide, choose a strategy, etc.). This is done using Design Sheets.

Implement Your Self-Evolutionary Template

Subjective experience which has been implanted in a Self-Evolutionary template is then embedded in your conscious and unconscious awareness using "spatial associations." This is an excellent way to involve both hemispheres of the brain (and the rest of the body) as you schedule yourself for success.

SET for Success will help you feel and taste determination when you decide to.

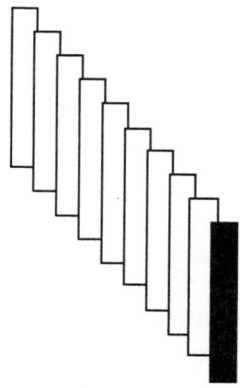

Appendix

Brain Function

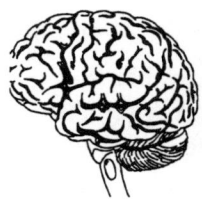

You can create subjective experience without knowing how the brain works, you've been doing it since you were a baby and most of the design of the Self-Evolutionary process comes from nature and common sense, but you can do a much better job if you know about the brain.

The brain is inside of the skull and has abut 1500 chemicals that change from second to second as electrical charges go up and down axons, dendrites, and across synapses carrying thoughts to the different parts of the brain. This is no small thing. R. M. Restak, MD, in *The Brain* explains:

> Each of the at least ten billion neurons in the human brain may have over a thousand synapses—points of contact

between nerve cells...The total number of connections within the vast network of the brain's neuronal system is truly astronomical—greater than the number of particles in the known universe.[1]

Its hard to imagine if this is true or not (even using both hands). I like to avoid the numbers by knowing that I have all of the connections that I need, for the rest of my life; all I need to develop my potential and then some.

Lateralization

We use both the left and right hemispheres of the brain to create subjective experience. Most of the time there is good communication between the two hemispheres but sometimes one hemisphere doesn't seem to know what the other is doing. It's best to have both hemispheres involved, as much as possible. This process uses spatial associations, a Self-Evolutionary template, and other design features to ensure a complete, unified experience.

The Left Hemisphere

Refer to Figure 2. The left hemisphere is the language hemisphere and is very important as Dr. Joseph explains:

It is through language and thought that we are able to manipulate the world, describe ourselves, make predictions about the future, and symbolize aspects of the past in verbal memory and in written form. Via these modalities, we are able to analyze and describe the world as we view it and to express ourselves in a multimodal, multidimensional fashion.[2]

And where in the brain does it take place? New research always suggests that brain functions are more complex than originally thought and of course that has to be the case. We are just beginning to learn how the brain functions. Let's look at some of the major players in the left hemisphere.

Broca's Area provides the syntax for the words we speak and hear. It's called *Broca's Expressive Speech Area* and is named for Paul Broca who first described it in 1861; it's one of the three members of the Language Axis described later. Broca's Area also excites the motor cortex that controls the vocal cords and other muscles creating the words that emanate from our mouths. I compare it to a grammar teacher.

People suffering from damage to this area (called Broca's Aphasia) are unable to understand or make grammatically complex sentences. Speech consists almost entirely of disjointed content words; worse than George Bush's "ain't gonna do it, been there" style of speaking.

The **Amygdala** is a conduit for information from the ear and the ancient cortical areas of the brain to the modern neocortex. The Amygdala is the stairs between the first floor and the second story addition.

The **Primary Auditory Area** (left side) is where auditory information is initially received (from the thalamus and amygdala) and analyzed before sharing it with Wernicke's Area and the Angular Gyrus (Figure 1). It also connects to the Primary Auditory Area (right side) for speech synthesis giving words both a logical and emotional meaning.

Wernicke's Area (*Wernicke's Receptive Language Area*) is where words are formed and is important both for decoding incoming speech sounds (words) "but also acts to verbally organize the temporal sequential order and the auditory-verbal associations of everything a person is planning to say."[3]

It was named for Carl Wernicke who first described it in 1874.

People who suffer from neurophysiological damage in this area (called Wernicke's Aphasia) are unable to understand the content words while listening and unable to produce meaningful sentences; their speech has grammatical structure but no meaning.

While we listen, speech information is transported from the Primary Auditory Area to Wernicke's area for evaluation of content words, then to Broca's area for analysis of syntax. In speech production, content words are selected by neural systems in Wernicke's area, grammatical refinements are added by neural systems in Broca's area, and then the information is sent to the motor cortex, which sets up the muscle movements for speaking.

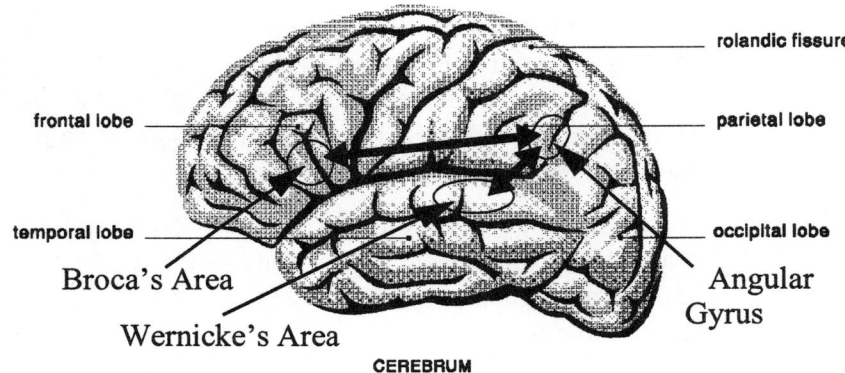

Figure 1: The Language Axis

The **Angular Gyrus** is connected to the same rope of fibers
that connects to Broca's area and Wernicke's area completing
the linguistic unit often called the "language axis." See Figure
1. Dr. Joseph explains the angular gyrus:

> The angular gyrus is uniquely situated so that the areas of
> the brain that process visual, tactile, and auditory
> information are at its borders, where they all
> intercommunicate. That is, the angular gyrus sits at the
> juncture where touch is processed in the parietal lobe,
> where visual analyses are performed in the occipital lobe,
> and where sounds are analyzed in the temporal lobe. It is in
> the angular gyrus that auditory, visual, and tactile
> sensations are combined to form a multimodal
> representation for what is being experienced...In other
> words, through its interconnections with various brain
> areas, the angular gyrus is able to call forth ideas and
> relevant associations and then link them together to help
> form concepts and categories.[4]

The Angular Gyrus is where complex associations are
performed allowing for the comprehension of abstract and
symbolic speech (from parables to the Theory of Relativity).

The most distinctive difference between humans and our
ancestors the apes is that we have an angular gyrus.

Associations are made in the angular gyrus in a "parallel
manner" (touch, visual, and sounds are combined) although the

way that we speak and listen is in a sequential manner, one word after another. This is just one of many ways that the brain functions in both a serial and parallel format; to our great advantage. "Her words shook the rhythm of my heart but her gaze and soft hair gave me images for a lifetime."

The Angular Gyrus (left side) is connected to the Angular Gyrus (right side) via the corpus callosum in order to give the rational experience created in the left hemisphere the emotional, melodic, spatial, perceptual, and movement qualities that are generated in the right hemisphere. The power of the angular gyrus in the left and right hemispheres is amazing and when combined with the other components of the brain and the rest of the nervous system, is astounding.

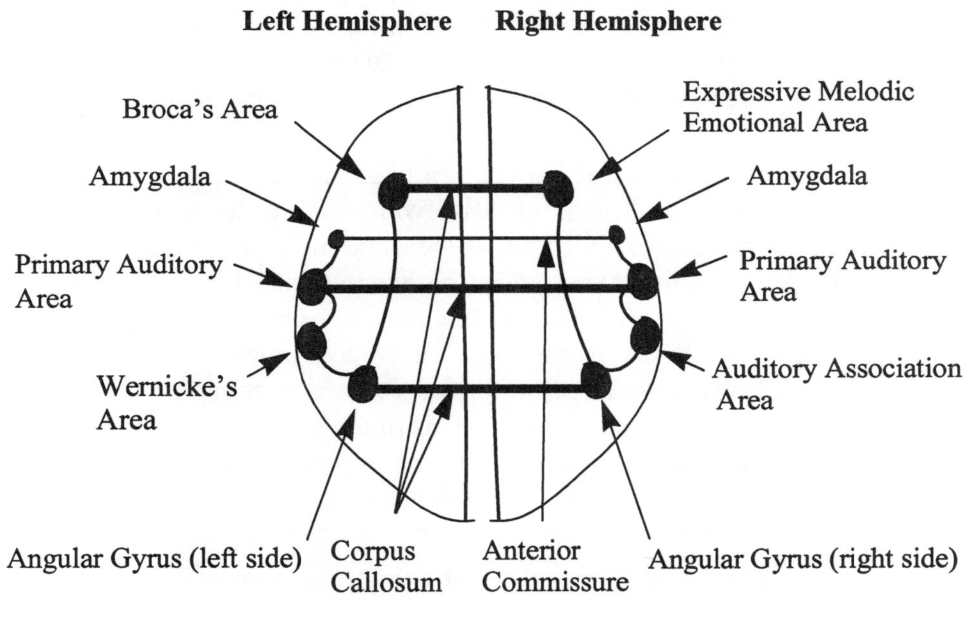

Left Hemisphere   Right Hemisphere

Figure 2: Brain Function

The Right Hemisphere

Refer to Figure 2. Dr. Joseph explains the right hemisphere:

> Among modern humans, the right half of the brain is responsible for discerning distance, depth, and movement; for recognizing environmental and animal sounds; and for controlling most aspects of emotion, social behavior, and

body language, as well as the capacity to sing, dance, chase or throw something with accuracy, and run without falling or bumping into things. The visual, emotional, hallucinatory, and hypnagogic aspects of dreaming are also associated with right-brain mental activity.[5]

The right hemisphere is more creative than the left. It's an excellent companion, associate, copartner with the left hemisphere, and is very powerful when creating a strong desire to be successful.

We have all of the tools we need to be successful, it's just a matter of creating, enhancing, and associating subjective experience (images, sounds, and feeling) and then projecting it into the future in a compelling manner. We think in a temporal-sequential manner, one thought after another, just as we speak one word after another. The parallel processing that the brain performs routinely while feeling, seeing, and hearing is in some ways more powerful than temporal-sequential processing but how do you program it? In a temporal-sequential manner. Let's see how.

We can't be consciously aware of all of the aspects of a successful endeavor, at the same time, so we embed the subjective experience (that we implant in a Self-Evolutionary template) deep in our memory, our unconscious. Since we want to be programmed for success in the most complete, powerful manner possible, we need to engage both hemispheres of the brain as much as possible. The right hemisphere is a powerful mate to the left and visa versa. The spatial associations consummate the marriage.

The Melodic-Emotional Language Axis

A complete explanation for brain function is a long way off and would not be within the scope of this book. Since we want to create subjective experience (how we see, feel, and hear) with power and determination, let's look at the Melodic-Emotional Language Axis which consists of:

1. the Expressive-Melodic Emotional Area,

2. the Auditory Association Area, and

3. the Angular Gyrus (right side) as shown in Figure 2.

This axis is similar to the language axis of the left hemisphere and is explained by Dr. Joseph.

> Although left-brain speech eventually becomes preeminent in the expression of verbal thoughts and ideas, the right brain is dominant for melodic and emotional speech, perception, and expression. The right brain remains dominant for one's ability to discern and impart meaning, context, sincerity, and emotional intent.[6]

The **Expressive-Melodic Emotional Area** is responsible for melody and emotion just as Broca's area is responsible for the framing of words and then having the vocal cords speak them. The right hemisphere enables us to sing with feeling. The "Language Axis" of the left hemisphere and the "Melodic-Emotional Language Axis" of the right hemisphere are connected via the corpus callosum allowing for the mixing of words and music (from Joe Cocker and Neil Young to Placido Domingo). A fiery speech on the Senate floor comes from both hemispheres of the brain; the fire from the right and the logic (if there is any) from the left.

The **Amygdala** is a conduit for information from the ear and the ancient cortical areas of the brain to the modern neocortex. The Amygdala is the stairs between the first floor and the second story addition.

The **Primary Auditory Area** (right side) is where auditory information is initially received (from the thalamus and Amygdala) and then analyzed and shared with the Auditory Association Area. It focuses on tone of voice, voice inflection, and emotional content and then adds it to the rational interpretation of the Primary Auditory Area (left side). This enables the comprehension of speech with emotion and melody.

The **Auditory Association Area** is the region where "complex auditory associations are performed and where the comprehension of speech...or environmental-melodic, emotional sound occurs."[7] This is where the sound of taps is associated with death and loss and where the theme from Rocky is associated with victory.

In summary, the **Angular Gyrus** (right side) is connected to the a rope of fibers that connects to the "Expressive-Melodic Emotional Area" and the "Auditory Association Area" and completes the "Melodic-Emotional Language Axis." It connects directly, via the corpus callosum, to the Angular Gyrus of the left hemisphere so that the logical experience created in the left hemisphere (the Language Axis) is combined with the emotional, melodic, visual, spatial attributes of the right hemisphere. These are a lot of technical words and ideas and they seem complicated; they add up to logic and emotional power for success.

Making a Difference

How can we provide more power to the subjective experiences we create? How can we see, hear, and feel our goals with greater clarity to give them more authority? We could try music. The left brain provides the necessary temporal-sequential punctuation with words and rhythm as the right hemisphere provides the melody and tune.

> Auditory information is received in the primary auditory area, as well as within the amygdala of the limbic system (and other limbic areas). Emotional and related characteristics are discerned, comprehended, and/or assigned to the sounds perceived. When one is speaking emotionally or is singing, or cursing, this information is transferred from the temporal-parietal and limbic areas to the right frontal area, which mediates the expression of the information...Through interaction with the right angular gyrus, these brain areas combine the sounds into a pleasing gestalt, which is then transmitted to the right frontal area, where the melody is vocally expressed. These areas are interconnected by a rope of nerve fibers, the arcuate fasciculus. If the left brain desires, it can provide the necessary temporal-sequential punctuation so as to provide the words and rhythm and thus sing along. However, it can also engage in foot or finger tapping if it cannot remember the words.[8]

Converting a Self-Evolutionary template to music may be for experienced musicians but don't be intimidated. A series of lyrics that can be hummed (like you did your ABC's) or maybe just a series of statements that rhyme, like a poem, can add zest to your subjective experience (that defines your goal). Any time that we combine an image with dialogue and feeling we are using both sides of the brain; creating a multidimensional, subjective experience.

How Associations Work

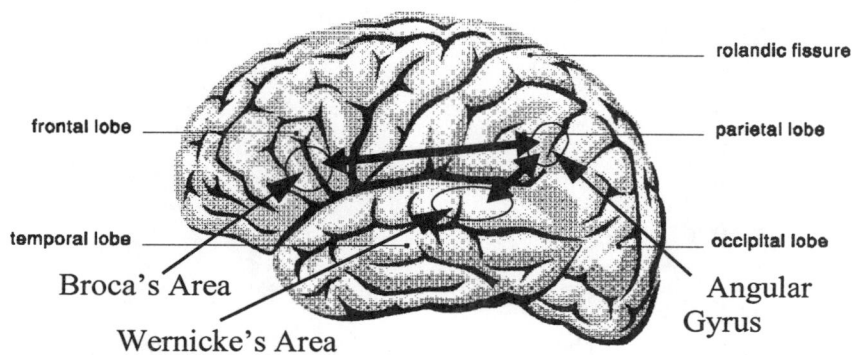

You can make associations without knowing how you do it just like you can drive a car without knowing how the engine works. Do you want to be an operator or an expert, it's up to you?

Here's how associations work. The angular gyrus in the left hemisphere, the part of the brain that differentiates us from apes, is at the boundaries of the parietal lobe (touch) the occipital lobe (vision) and the temporal lobe (sound) and makes complex associations that have been created elsewhere available for assimilation. Because the three areas listed above overlap (share neurons) within the angular gyrus, it acts like a mixer, it combines information from all three modalities. But this is only part of the system, the angular gyrus (rational left hemisphere) mixes information with the angular gyrus and associated components of the (emotional, melodic right hemisphere).

Subjective experience can be imagined, remembered, brought into conscious awareness and then associated (linked) to any of the five sensory modalities because when "activated, this area acts to transfer from other neocortical and old cortical regions whatever associations are needed."[9] A subjective experience can be associated to a part of the body; your right ear lobe, for instance. To recreate the subjective experience the association point can be "fired off" by holding the right ear lobe again.

Endnotes

1. R. M. Restak, MD *The Brain* (New York: Bantam Books,1984).

2. R. Joseph, *The Right Brain and the Unconscious* (New York: Plenum Press, 1992).

3. Ibid.

4. Ibid.

5. Ibid.

6. Ibid.

7. Ibid.

8. Ibid.

9. R. Joseph, The Naked Neuron (New York: Plenum Press, 1993).

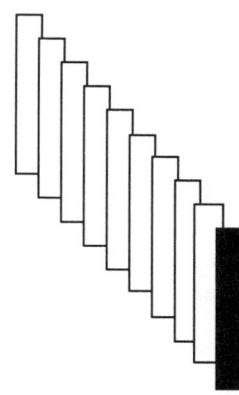

About the Author

My Mission is to develop my potential as a human being and help others, who are interested, to do the same. This is the best way that I know of to participate in the evolution of humankind.

David A. Jacobi

David A. Jacobi has had a lifelong interest in how the mind works. He obtained a B.A. in Psychology from Rutgers in the 70s. He also wrote plays and poetry as he tried to resolve issues left over from a dysfunctional childhood.

In the 80s, his writing turned to nonfiction including computer manuals and technical writing but there was always the underlying issue of how to be successful after starting off so badly.

In the 90s, he has been studying evolution, the brain, Neuro-Linguistic Programming (NLP), and life. He says that he wrote this book for himself: "I needed it. The other books didn't go far enough for me."

He has a keen interest in beliefs, decisions, and strategies; how they function and interact with each other and hopes to pursue this interest with other interested parties.

He also has a keen interest in how we are going to evolve in the future with the tremendous advances in technology and the exponential increase in information.

His interest in the mind has led him in many directions from psychology to spiritual paths; from computers to the Internet; from new age to history.

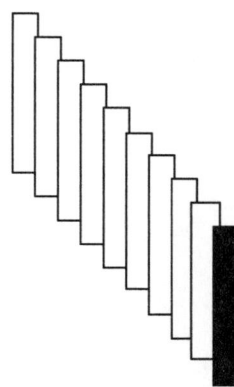

Feedback

All feedback is appreciated. How to improve the book, other methods for success, technical information on the brain (especially how beliefs, decisions, and strategies work and interact) is most welcome. If you send a review of the book or provide information, please indicate if I have permission to use it; with proper credit, of course.

Order this book using the directions on the back cover. Call BookMasters to order a copy of the book, only. They have no information about the book itself.

Direct all questions about the book to:

David A. Jacobi
267 Carlton Ave.
Piscataway, NJ 08854-3056
(732) 968-1473

www.setforsuccess.com
book@setforsuccess.com

Conventional wisdom says that if you "really believe" you can do something, *you can. SET for Success* teaches you to really believe.

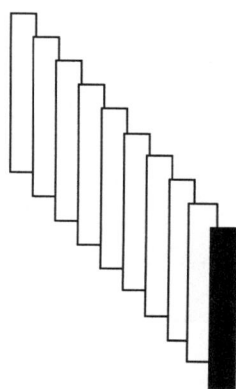

Order Form

Mail a copy of this form (include reverse side) to one of the following:

For an autographed copy (U.S. only), send order with check (make out to David A. Jacobi). Include instructions for autograph.	For a regular copy. Also contact BookMasters for information about sales outside of the United States.
David A. Jacobi 267 Carlton Ave. Piscataway, NJ 08854-3056 david@setforsuccess.com www.setforsuccess.com	BookMasters, Inc. PO Box 388 Ashland, OH 44805 Order can be faxed to 1 419 281-6883 or phone toll free to 1 888 822-6657 (include credit card information) also order at www.bookmasters.com
SET for Success $29.95	
Sales tax as applicable	
S&H $4.95	
Total:	

(Shipping information on the reverse side)

Mail *SET for Success* to:	
Name:	
Address:	
City:	
State:	
Country:	
Zip Code:	
Telephone:	
Email:	
Website:	
Autograph instructions if being ordered from author:	

180

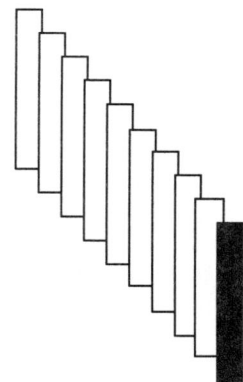

Index

A

A Good Goal 90
About the Author 175
Actor's View 115
Amygdala 167, 171
Analyze the Results 24, 82, 123
Angular Gyrus 168, 171
Anthony Robbins 15
Appendix 165
Associate Subjective Experience 64
Assumptions 70
Auditory Association Area 171

B

Beliefs, Decisions, and Strategies 17
Believe 24, 81, 97
Bipedalism 28
Bipedalism and temporal-sequential
    activities 36
Body awareness 43
Brain Function 165
Brain Size 35
Broca's Area 166

C

Choose a Strategy 24, 81, 109
Churchill 12
Concepts 39
Conscious awareness 37
Conscious Awareness/Unconscious
    Awareness 38

Cradle of Civilization 2
Creating Subjective Experience 51
Cuban Missile Crisis 109
cutting the corpus callosum 44
cybernetic model 14

D

death awareness 32
Decide 24, 81, 103
Decision Analysis 104
Definition of Beliefs 49
Definition of Decisions 50
Definition of Intuition 50
Definition of Projections 50
Definition of Questions 49
Derived gains 93
Design Your Self-Evolutionary
    Template 87
Director's View 114
Dividing Time and Space 52
DNA 2, 8
Donald Norman 42
Dr. R. Joseph 15, 52
Dr. R. W. Sperry 44
Draw Your Time Concept 69

E

Einstein 12
Enhance Your Feelings 60
Enhancing Subjective Experience 59

Entertain Ideas 23, 80, 88
Epilog 134
Establishing Your Time Concept 69
Expressive-Melodic Emotional
    Area 171

F
Favorite Sensory System 57
Feedback 177
five senses 35

G
Generate Good Internal Dialogue 62
Generate Strong Images 62

H
Harry Jerison 35
Homo Erectus 30
How to Use This Book 19

I
Ideas in Space 51
Implement the Template 84
Implement Your Self-Evolutionary
    Template 129
Implementing a Template 132
In a Secure Manner 91
Influence, The Psychology of
    Persuasion 20

J
John F. Kennedy 109

K
kids killing kids 6

L
Language 68
Language and Senses 33
language window 8
Lateralization 166
Learning 39
Learning and Thinking 38
Left-Brain Awareness 42
Look Backward 25
Look Forward 11, 181
Look Inward 37
Look to the Future 20

Look to the Past 25
Loom of Language 33

M
Make the Projection 115
Mark McGwires 6
Maxwell Maltz 14
maya 2
Melodic-Emotional Language
    Axis 170
Mental Tools 47
Model of the World 35
Modern Humans 32
Monitoring Thoughts 48
Morton Hunt 42
Multiple Thoughts 48
My Responsibility 13

N
Nikola Tesla 47
no failures, only feedback 72

O
occipital lobe 168
Of Your Own Volition 93
One Thing at a Time 49
Order Form 179
original intention 71
Original Intentions/Derived Gains 92
Origins Reconsidered 28
Overview 77

P
Parallel Processing 45
parietal lobe 168
Part One 19, 21
Part Two 19
Pavlov's dogs 30
Perform Rehearsal 24, 82, 120
possible for all 71
Power of the Unconscious 44
Primary Auditory Area 167, 171
Project into the Future 70
Project Subjective Experience 67
Project the Effects 24, 82, 118
Project the Outcome 24, 81, 114
Psycho-Cybernetics 14, 15

Q

Qualify an Idea 24, 81, 90

R

Reality Score Card 127, 133
reference experience 44
Repetition Counts 123
reticular formation 5, 38
Richard Leakey 28, 35
Right-Brain Awareness 43
Robert B. Cialdini 20
Rubber Meets the Road 125

S

sabotaging yourself 13
Sammy Sosas 6
Self Esteem 14
Self Help Books 15
Self-Evolutionary Components 80,
    132
Self-Evolutionary Process 83
Self-Evolutionary template 13
Sensory Adjustments 59
Sensory Based 94
Sensory Modalities 53
sensory modalities 49
Sensory Sequencing 58
SET for Success 11
short term memory 39
Simple Associations 65
social behavior 169
Spatial Associations 66
State of Mind 131
stuff of success 44
Subjective Experience 53
Success or Failure 14

T

teach reading 8
tectonic plates 28
Television 5
television commercials 5
temporal lobe 168
Temporal-Sequential Activities 31
temporal-sequential activities 32
temporal-sequential process 17
Terrence Deacon 44

The Big Bang 26
The Calendar 67
The Earth 27
the five senses 34
The Great Rift Valley 29
The Left Hemisphere 166
The Process Further Defined 45, 72
The Right Brain and the
    Unconscious 15
The Right Hemisphere 169
The Self-Evolutionary Process 18
The Solar System 27
The Universe 26
Thinking 40
This Book 17
Thomas Edison's choice 47
Thoughts About Change 19
Thoughts are Valuable 20
Time 67
Time and space 12
time and space 46
Tony Robbins 83
tool making 32
Truman 17
two hemispheres in our brain 46

U

Unconscious 38
Unconscious awareness 38
Use a Reference Belief 99
Using Positive Language 94

V

View Time and Envision Time 69
violent kids 6
Visualization of Time 67

W

We are all connected 72
We are human evolution 2
We are success 2
We prefer consistency 7
Wernicke's Area 167
What are Beliefs? 98
What is Consciousness? 37
What is Reality? 87
What is Success? 78
What is Your Reality? 11

Thank You   Very Much